TRAVELLER

Observations from an American in Exile

MICHAEL KATAKIS

FOREWORD BY MICHAEL PALIN

BURTON & PARK PUBLISHERS
SAN FRANCISCO
PARIS

iv   TRAVELLER

For Kris my 'True North'

And for

T.E. Lawrence
*Who helped a solitary little boy dream
of deserts and far away places*

With best wishes

June 29, 2009

Arriving at each new city, the traveler finds again a past
of his that he did not know he had: the foreignness of
what you no longer are or no longer possess lies in wait
for you in foreign unposessed places.

Italo Calvino
Invisible Cities

Published in the United States by
Burton & Park Publishers

Copyright © Michael Katakis 2009
ISBN 978-0-9820007-0-0

Cover: Market Day, Sierra Leone and all book photographs, copyright © Michael Katakis

Design: Takigawa Design, Monterey, California
Printed in China

The author is grateful for permission to quote from the following:
Excerpt from *Invisible Cities* © Estate of Italo Calvino.
Quote from *The Dark Heart of Italy* © Tobias Jones.

The British spelling of Traveller, used in the title is an homage to the British travelers and explorers
who filled the author with wonder first as a young boy and then, as an adult.

First Edition

Burton & Park Publishers
P.O. Box 277
Carmel, California 93921-0277

For more information go to:
www.burtonparkbooks.net
www.mkatakis.org

TABLE OF CONTENTS

FOREWORD

I 've known Michael for a few years now, ever since he provided invaluable help for a television series I was making on Ernest Hemingway. I had been drawn to Hemingway, not just because he had written boldly and with a fresh voice about the eternal themes of love and war, courage and cowardice, but because he remained, throughout his life, consumed with interest in a world beyond his own country. Through our collaboration I quickly discovered that Michael and I shared not only a respect for Hemingway, but a respect for Hemingway's thirst for travel.

Hemingway, having effected this introduction, left us to get on with it and for nearly ten years now we have been sharing our delight and despair at the wonderful world we live in. I say, "sharing" and immediately feel somewhat compromised. Michael is a great correspondent. A far better correspondent than I shall ever be. He writes letters, proper letters composed in pen and ink, from wherever he is in the world, whenever he feels moved to write. Scribbled perhaps in a train or at table after a particularly good meal, Michael's letters, and many are reproduced here, exult in discovery. His delight is our delight.

Fortunately, he keeps a journal as well. As in his letters, fleeting moments and sudden glimpses are as powerfully evocative as his longer, more considered entries. Nothing is wasted, and nothing is too trivial for him to note, which I think is so important. Once we start censoring what we see, filing it away under weighty or significant, we miss the moment. In both his letters and in his journal, Michael has an infectious ability to sense the essence of a place and transmit it to the reader. Whether on the dusty roads of Sierra Leone, in a café on the Bosporus, in a Chinese village without a map, in Dallas, Texas or on the Paris Metro, he makes a place for us beside him.

Michael has two other vital qualities for a good traveller. Curiosity and a conscience. I've seen his curiosity in action. He goes up to people, says hello and asks what they're doing and where they're from. And does it with such charm and obvious good intent that soon he has friends around him like the Pied Piper had children.

At the same time, he worries and he cares. Frustration, disillusion and indignation burst out of these pages, undisguised and deeply felt. He loves the world and he can't bear to see it fall into the hands of those who are out for personal gain at the expense of others. He looks at himself as honestly as he looks at the rest of the world. Learning about people means being prepared to trade your own experience, as he does with a moving and poetic allusion to his mother's death, a fine description of accompanying his father back to the birthplace he hasn't seen for forty years, or his first delightful feelings on meeting Kris, the woman to whom he has dedicated this book.

In short, Traveller contains all the reasons why I value Michael's friendship and the pleasures I've gained from it. Technically, he is enormously gifted. His photographs are peerless. The landscapes have a cool, serene beauty and his portraits convey joy and dignity in equal measure. He has an open mind and a warm heart. He is always discovering, never presuming, always learning, never preaching. Which is why he's worth listening to, and why the implication of his subtitle, "*Observations From An American in Exile*" is both sad and timely.

Michael's way of looking at the world is diametrically opposed to those who believe in world domination, whether it be religious, economic or technological. A book like this, which so vividly celebrates the fine detail of life, makes the casual violence of our times all the more abhorrent and shameful.

For me, the message of "*Traveller*", and I'm sure Michael would deny providing anything as clumsy as a message, is that pain and suffering is much less easy to inflict if someone is looking at you. Michael forces us to look people in the face. To remind ourselves that every human life is a mirror of our own.

Traveller is the work of a decent honourable man in a world where the deceitful and dishonourable have far too much influence. If you want to be reassured that the word humanity still means something, look inside.

Michael Palin
London

INTRODUCTION

Journal entry
1 October 2005
Istanbul

How could I have known then with no maps acquired and my bags not yet packed that my journey had already begun?

I am standing on a bank of the Bosporus watching the meandering river make its way toward the Black Sea. Behind me lay Europe, ahead Asia and over a period of days now, in this place memories, my memories have gently intruded themselves upon me. I remember.

The bedroom was not large though at the time it seemed so. Through Venetian blinds the sliced summer sunlight made patterns on the bed where my mother lay dying. She was going on a long journey I was told so I waited in that room with my mother and with death wanting to know them before they left. I did not look away.

At school a November morning and a passing sensation, perhaps that of departure. I ran from the schoolyard past the Dutch bakery and Chinese laundry, down familiar streets with leafless trees. Running, then faster, blurring landscape and a feeling of flight as in dreams. Past the Wagon Wheel diner and Patio theatre back to the room where the autumn light, diffuse now made patterns on the bare mattress.

The tools of a traveler are compass and map. They calculate distances covered and destinations sought but cannot measure the consequences of experiences on a human heart. I remember.

To the little girl in West Africa with tuberculosis whom I could not save, I think of you often and I am sorry. To the Chinese farmer and his family who gave me their bed and laughed at my attempts to plant rice. To the Frenchman on the *Pont des Arts* who offered me a glass of wine when the war began and to the South Korean soldier who broke into laughter after tasting a milkshake for the first time. To the angry Palestinian in Chicago, the courageous Muslim woman in France and the exhausted fireman in St. Paul's chapel in New York days after the 'horror'. To the young man with his head in the stars who I betrayed with the truth and to my friend, Sahr, who protected me and whom I hope has survived the civil war.

Finally to my dear father, who stayed and whetted my appetite for the world.

To all of those and many more I owe a debt. If they ever have occasion to read these words and recognize themselves, I hope that they will agree that I kept their trust and my word and I did not look away.

Journal entry
18 July 1988
Sierra Leone, West Africa: Kainkordu

Sahr woke me early to say that someone had come. Half asleep I walked into the outdoor room to find a fresh pail of river water. I always take time for the morning bucket bath, sometimes luxuriating for too long because it allows me the only time to be alone. This morning I was annoyed at having to rush. Someone from Kainkordu needed or wanted something I thought or just wished to sit silent on the veranda, sometimes for hours, visiting in that strange Kono way to which I can never grow accustomed.

On the veranda sat a small nicely dressed man in his twenties I'd guessed. He rose to greet me with an extended hand and held a large box in the other. He seemed familiar and at first did not speak. I apologized for not having tea but offered him some filtered water which he took and drank quickly. I offered more, which he accepted.

"Do we know each other," I asked.

"No, but I...." His eyes looked behind me as Kris came out and joined us. He rose again and I was about to repeat my question when Kris said, "We met in the lorry park in Koidu did we not?"

"Yes, that is right. We met when you were trying to get transport upcountry to Kainkordu."

"You have traveled quite a way," I said. "Is there something we can do for you?" He became nervous and agitated, and, after what seemed a long time, Kris began to excuse herself when he quickly and, somewhat desperately, interrupted, "I have come to ask you questions."

With that he set the large box on the table opening it carefully so as not to further stress the already broken spine.

The contents, which he began to, and there is no other word for it, tenderly remove, were drawings and charts of the stars as well as old and yellowed newspaper clippings with stories about the American space program. There were stories about Mercury, Apollo and the names of some astronauts including John Glenn which were circled in red. The young man's hand drawings of Saturn and Mars were remarkable and on some of the pages there were a series of equations that I took to mean latitude and longitude but could not be sure. He went on turning page after page. In another place and time he would have been a student or perhaps a professor of astronomy I thought. His passion for the subject was startling and I could see that Kris, too, was amazed by the quality and sheer volume of his writings and drawings.

I told him that this was fantastic but my compliment was either ignored or not heard as he arranged more pages on the table. He then asked me his questions. They were about propulsion systems and temperatures on planets. Questions about Haley's comet and other astronauts' names and how the space program had developed after he had lost track. How far was the end of the galaxy and how long would it take to reach it and then questions about the theory of relativity. I was dumbfounded and could only manage a silly, insecure smile in response, and then, I made one of the greatest mistakes of my life. I told the truth. I said, "You have studied this so much and it's amazing but I'm afraid that you know much more about this than I do. I am learning from you and I can't answer your questions. I simply don't know."

The look on his face cut deep and in an instant I realized that he had not come for facts at all. He had come for new words to dream by. Perhaps my words would have carried him until August or September and maybe well past. He might have lay in the tall grass at night staring at the stars remembering the veranda where we had talked and ponder what was said. Perhaps he would have fallen into deep sleeps and dreamt of stars and in those dreams he might have taken flight far from his life of questions with no answers and loneliness. But that was not to be for I made the terrible mistake of admitting my ignorance and removing myself from our delicate charade.

I learned in that moment, when I took everything from him, the importance of lying, not merely telling an untruth but lying, with passion and flourish like an actor on a stage claiming to know that which they do not know, for the lie that keeps hope and dreams intact is preferable to a truth that removes them. Lies and truths are easy to come by but dreams that sustain people through difficult lives are not. I wish I could take back the day.

Journal entry
9 October 2004
Paris

It is an overcast day with an on and off again rain. I walk down into the Metro and enter a crowded car heading for Raspail. My eyes immediately turn to a young man reading. He holds his book two inches from his eyes which are magnified through thick lenses that have an additional lens attached to the lower part of the heavy Buddy Holly glasses. The small book is about music and symphony *(La Musique et La Symphonie)*. The eyes race back and forth but surely he can only be seeing one word at a time. His tongue peers slightly out of the side of his mouth then a smile, it's joyful, nearly a laugh. I see part of a page, musical notes. Can he hear the music? A savant? He is taking it in fast seemingly racing ahead of the darkness for the darkness is coming. Relishing the book his facial expressions are everchanging: joy, struggle, fear, wonder, excitement, expectation, disability, nobility, youth and age. I cannot take my eyes off him and am grateful that he is unaware of my staring. The train stops and in the window's reflection I see he squints and struggles to see the station names. I think he has missed his stop. He tries to stand and again looks at the book and sits down. Stop after stop he sits there smiling, lost in the pages. As I stepped into the street, I was aware of the cool, clean air. The rain had stopped and the colors of the city seemed bright and alive in the dull, soft light. I, too, felt alive and hopeful and grateful for all of the small, wonderful things.

A BEAUTIFUL ANKLE

Letter
Dennis High, Carmel, California
19 July 2004
Santa Margherita, Italy

Crossing the street I turned to see the lovely young woman with milk chocolate skin on her teal Vespa looking at me as though I were young. She drove away and the wind picked up a bit of her skirt revealing a beautiful ankle. I watched. She never looked back.

TRANSVESTITES FOR BUSH

Journal entry
20 March 2003
Paris

The cab driver had a five o'clock shadow on his/her face and a pretty gingham dress, peach color. How odd I thought, wearing a summer dress on a cool winter night. We engaged in conversation and she had a deep gravelly voice. He/she talked some politics and she/he denounced President Chirac and praised President Bush. This seemed very strange to me. In a heavy accent she/he said, "Bush number one, Chirac zero."

I thought that perhaps the Bush administration should be informed seeing that this support from a transvestite might suggest larger support. 'Transvestites for Bush' might be the new battle cry.

Journal entry
27 August 1988
Kainkordu, Sierra Leone

What a remarkable day. Sahr and I are walking to Mangema past the large tree. It is already very hot. Sahr is a fine man and very good company and has one of those sparkling minds that take in the world. We talk about many things and I am surprised when he tells me about his great grandfather who fought the British with his 'invisible cloak'.

"This is why the British could not find him," Sahr tells me. "He would enter a room with the British in pursuit and then cover himself with the cloak and disappear."

"Sahr that's ridiculous. You know that's impossible," I say.

Sahr looks at me with determination and a bit of exasperation and retells his story with more flourish and even more remarkable hand gestures. We walked on and I do not recall how it came up but I told Sahr that the United States had landed men on the moon. With that Sahr begins to laugh so hard that he falls into the tall grass on the side of the road. Annoyed, I raise my voice over his laughter and say, "But it's true, they did land on the moon."

Sahr's laughter grows so loud and infectious that soon we're both laughing uncontrollably. Women walking the rough road barefoot with large bundles balanced on their heads pause and stare at the sight of us laughing and start to laugh themselves.

There we were, both on the ground, certain the other crazy and each of us knowing what we had said was 'true'. Never has an education in culture been more enjoyable.

TANGO

Journal entry
14 May 2008
Paris

I have discovered that there is an evening of Tango somewhere in Paris. I find the old building on the city outskirts and, as I enter, music is playing in the distance. Entering the dimly lit room with the music that beckons, expressionless couples twirl around the floor. There is a bit of fascism in the air and I wonder if 1920's Buenos Aires was like this?

Walking across the room I see that people are seated around three of the four walls. A woman, with a black pageboy, red lips, a black dress, and spiked heels stares at me. She looks beautiful, and dangerous.

I sit down by the back wall, concentrating on the feet moving past me, trying to see a pattern in the dance. After ten minutes I can see no pattern, and try for another ten. The couples are mesmerizing and the room is getting warm.

I see the dangerous woman with red lips get up and walk toward me. She sits to my left facing forward.

"Would you like to dance?" She asks.

"I am watching, trying to find a pattern."

"There is no pattern," she says still looking forward. "So, tell me what you see."

"The best I can determine is that the man builds the house and the woman decorates it."

"That is a good description of Tango," she says. "So, you like to watch."

"Yes"

"Tell me watcher, do you ever do?"

"I do. Sometimes."

She laughs ever so slightly and it seems to me that at any other time and in any other place this conversation would be part of a bad Hollywood script but it really is happening and it feels real. These are eccentric people who Tango in different parts of the city every week and they are wonderfully bizarre. The room is getting hotter.

"So you do, do, from time to time." she continues. "That's a relief for a person cannot live by watching alone. I like to do, but I do like to be watched, too."

"I suspected that. You are an attractive woman who seems dangerous and that is always appealing to watchers and doers alike."

"Dangerous. How do you mean?" she asks, finally turning and looking at me.

"This is an odd conversation." I say.

"Odd how?"

As I'm about to answer, a small Asian man stands before her and asks if she would like to dance. She stands, towering over the petite man when, in an instant, he holds her. His body language changes and taking charge, begins to effortlessly steer the tall woman around the room. For a moment I watch them but she never looks in my direction. Looking again at the passing feet, I still cannot see a pattern.

I HOPE THE DOG WINS

Journal entry
12 October 2006
Tangier, Morocco

I am wandering around the docks in Tangier. I have been watching six dock boys pestering a dog that has been minding its own business, seemingly waiting for someone. Finally, one boy takes a stick and pokes the dog as the other boys laugh. The boy does it again and the dog barks. The boy starts to imitate the bark but the dog turns away. He then walks to another part of the street but the boys follow and throw the stick at him, hitting him on the head. The dog has had enough. With remarkable speed the animal runs after the boys. At one point I see him grab a piece of pants from one of his now, panicked tormentors. The police are watching this and laughing. The dog, very aggressive now, chases one boy to a chain link fence and the boy, with nearly super human strength, leaps sideways over the fence landing hard on his elbow, which yields a cracking sound. He yells in pain. The dog turns and takes off for the others. One boy amazingly jumps in the water and another runs on top of a car. Now the police come over and tell the boy to get off the car. It may be OK to be ripped apart by a dog in Tangier, but clearly it is not all right to jump on a car. I must confess I am cheering for the dog. I suspect the police are, too, as they walk by the animal and pat his head. The dog settles down and then calmly walks back to where he was before. I like Tangier.

LEAVING AMERICA

Letter
Michael Palin, London
4 April 2004
Paris

Dear Michael,

I suspect that you are puzzled by my decision to leave the United States for a time so I thought that I would try to explain my frustration and decision. As you know, I have had a number of serious complaints about my country for some time now and felt I could no longer just sit and complain. Seeing that I am not a wealthy man, the decision carried some hardships but thankfully Kris and I were in agreement as to the complaints and the remedy. I do hope that it will be temporary.

At the time of this writing, I am sitting in the lobby of a hotel in Paris. Behind the polished front desk a man is on the phone. His tone suggests a lingering affection or, perhaps, regret. I think it is an old lover. The one-way conversation drifts in and around me and I think about my country and how similar my feelings are to the changing tone of the man's voice. At first there is tenderness in the exchange, then frustration and a brief flash of anger. The muted second voice is raised and then faintly heard through the phone sobbing. The man's voice again turns tender.

I am an American. There is no changing that nor would I wish to and there was a time when we were in love, before the lying and deceit. A time when the world was young and everything seemed true and forever.

My relationship with my country is not dissimilar to that of the man and the mysterious woman on the phone. Like old lovers we know each other too well and there was no place left for our failings to hide.

We became infuriated with each other, she with me, because of my dissent, and me with her because of the lying and criminality done in my name.

To leave one's country and friends and the ones you love is always difficult but that difficulty is compounded when a loss of hope and belief are also left behind. While Bush and Cheney, cowards and opportunists of the worst kind, were the last straw on the proverbial camel, my disaffection had been growing for sometime.

My liberal friends put much faith in Clinton and could not bring themselves to admit that his recklessness had contributed much to where we find ourselves today. In the end he was a huckster having a good time and I grew tired of everyone waiting for the next political Messiah and using the nonappearance of said deity as an excuse for their, and my own, inaction. You know my feelings on critical thinking; Socratic questioning and stoicism that I wish America would embrace. The immediate benefit from such a philosophy might be a more reflective and intelligent citizenry which is desperately needed now. My naiveté aside we both know it isn't going to happen.

I am not anti-American, how could I be? What I am, however, is anti the people who have diminished the potential of what America could be because of personal greed and careerism of the most grotesque kind. After the election and the attacks Gore Vidal told me regarding the Bush administration, that, "The greatest criminal class in United States history had just ascended to the White House." At the time I thought his comments over the top, but now, sadly, I find that Mr. Vidal was engaged in understatement.

What was I to do then with the liars pushing us into war with a country that did not attack us and watching as Americans and others died while others inside and outside of government profited from that war? Perhaps the definition of treason should be expanded to those predatory capitalists, government officials and religious zealots who treat ordinary lives as something expendable in pursuit of their own increased profit and power. There were those on the left who, while not contributing to substantive debate and elucidation, wrote books about the 'liar's lies' and made a good penny out of their efforts. It seems that both sides have found the tearing apart of the country profitable. Increasingly I was watching my country evolving into a non-country, and becoming a giant store where everything was for sale: every principal, ethic and friend. A place where Americans were increasingly reduced to nothing more than a cash crop and with each misplaced step a bit more of our humanity and potential lost. What was I to do then, sit at home, pay taxes and turn away? I simply could not. And as many of my countrymen and women willingly allowed themselves to be manipulated, and the supposed press did nearly nothing that approached courage in doing their jobs (except for the brave Susan Sontag), the country seemed to slip into a football game mentality but, of course, the stakes were much higher. Not to fear. I gather none of Bush's, Cheney's nor immediate family members of congressmen, senators, corporate heads or fundamentalist religious leaders would serve or die. Oddly, they, like the all-purpose boogieman, Bin Laden, (who is never mentioned now) got others to die for their twisted visions and, dare I say, profit. Those who never sacrificed nor served their country trashed the reputations of those who had by lying and depicting 'them' as cowards and the public, with the help of news organizations bought it. It is disturbing to see one's countrymen and women so easily and willingly become fools and suckers. I felt like an impotent stranger in my own country.

The *New York Times* and *Washington Post*, useless. Fox television with its pro war propaganda and the silly Thomas Friedman's assessments. The press and corporate types and 'god fearing' Americans as well as the oh, so wrong Brits in America (CH) were talking and talking rubbish, moving us toward war with no evidence, none, and citizens on either side cheering that which coincided, not with truth, but rather their own prejudices and interests. From the news anchors and talk show hosts talking to the supposed 'insiders' that we were to believe were giving us the 'true gen' on television, and the ever arrogant Rumsfeld, the zealot Ashcroft and an ever growing assortment of despicable characters. What was I to do surrounded by such scoundrels and rank solipsistic careerists? I could not be part of the charade any longer and I used the only power left to me. My defiance.

I apologize very much for the tone of this letter for in the time we have known each other you and I have always talked about the wonders of the world and have always known the difference between politics and everything else, but I have turned the page. It is *Lorca* and it is 'five o'clock in the afternoon'.

The real sadness for me is as I travel the world I am often asked about the United States with a kind of hope and longing. When this occurs which is now less so, I think of my immigrant father and his dreams following those dreadful days on Crete in WWII. My father loved America but once told me that it was a delicate idea rather than a country. The noble idea he said was one of inclusion and a promise of an evolving society propelled by ideas, education and justice, in short, a place where everyone had a chance to improve, prosper and then contribute. He went on to say that if the 'idea' were betrayed or abandoned the betrayal would come from within and then the country would become nothing more than geography.

In London, at a hotel where I was staying, I spoke to a nice man who was the bartender. I believe that he was from Eastern Europe. He was saving to go to the United States and had some pretty wonderful dreams. His view of America was romanticized and I did not have the heart to set him straight. Besides it is people like him who will make the States better, and who am I to saddle him with my realities anyway? If I had the power to deport people, I would deport the likes of Bush, Cheney, the criminal corporate types and our own religious zealots who steer this plutocracy and let the likes of the bartender in. It is the look in people's eyes and their dream of America that breaks my heart for they have what I have lost: belief and faith.

So, what was I to do?

Love to you both,
Michael

Note: The preceding letter, though written privately later reminded me of one of T.E. Lawrence's public letters which appeared in the Sunday Times 22 August, 1920 under the heading, "Mesopotamia: The Truth about the Campaign." Here are some excerpts from that letter.

"The people of England have been led in Mesopotamia into a trap from which it will be hard to escape with dignity and honour. They have been tricked into it by a steady withholding of information. The Bagdad communiqués are belated, insincere, incomplete. Things have been far worse than we have been told, our administration more bloody and inefficient than the public knows. It is a disgrace

to our imperial record, and may soon be too inflamed for any ordinary cure. We are to-day not far from a disaster."

Worse than the Turks
"Our government is worse than the old Turkish system. They kept 14,000 local conscripts embodied, and killed a yearly average of two hundred Arabs in maintaining peace. We keep ninety thousand men, with aeroplanes, armoured cars, gunboats, and armoured trains. We have killed about ten thousand Arabs in this rising this summer. We cannot hope to maintain such an average: it is a poor country, sparsely peopled; but Abd el Hamid would applaud his masters, if he saw us working. We are told the object of the rising was political, we are not told what the local people want. It may be what the cabinet has promised them. A minister in the House of Lords said that we must have so many troops because the local people will not enlist...."

Cui Bono?
"We say we are in Mesopotamia to develop it for the benefit of the world. All experts say that the labour supply is the ruling factor in its development. How far will the killing of ten thousand villagers and townspeople this summer hinder the production of wheat, cotton and oil? How long will we permit millions of pounds, thousands of imperial troops, and tens of thousands of Arabs to be sacrificed on behalf of a form of colonial administration which can benefit nobody but its administrators?"

Additional Note:
Mr. Anthony Gurnee, a graduate of the United States Naval Academy, after reading Lawrence's letter, wrote to me to explain the meaning of the Latin ' Cui bono'. Mr. Gurnee writes: "Cui bono (To whose benefit, literally [being] good for whom) is a Latin adage that is used to suggest a hidden motive or to indicate that the party responsible for a thing may not be who it appears at first to be. With respect to motive, a public works project which is purported to benefit the city may have been initiated rather to benefit a favored campaign contributor with a lucrative contract.

Commonly the phrase is used to suggest that the person or people guilty of committing a crime may be found among those who have something to gain, chiefly with an eye toward financial gain. The party that benefits may not always be obvious or may have successfully diverted attention to a scapegoat, for example. The Roman orator and statesman Marcus Tullius Cicero, in his speech Pro

*Roscio Amerino, section 84, attributed the expression 'Cui bono?' to the Roman
consul and censor Lucius Cassius Longinus Ravilla. The famous Lucius Cassius,
whom the Roman people used to regard as a very honest and wise judge, was in
the habit of asking, time and again, 'To whose benefit?'*

*It is clear that given Lawrence's Oxford education that he was well versed
in Latin and when writing his letter to the Times was clear as to Cui bono's
meaning and implications.*

*If the reader would like to further research Cui bono or the Roman statesmen
mentioned, Anthony Gurnee stated that some of the material in his letter to me
was researched on Wikipedia as well as other sources.*

THE SAD GARDEN

Journal entry
18 August 1984
Crete, Greece

It is hard to believe that I am here with my father. He never spoke
about Greece. I think I understand now. I'll start at the beginning so as
to remember.

In May of 1941 people on Crete stared up at the sky as mushroom-
like shapes floated to earth. The invasion of Crete by the Germans had
begun. Among the witnesses were my father, his sister and brothers.
After the war my father immigrated to America and settled in Chicago.
When I think of my father, I think of his kindness and his gentle pride at
being self-made. He never spoke of those days on Crete. He never spoke
of anything that burdened him. My dreams took me to California but
every Sunday we spoke. I was surprised one Wednesday when the heavy
accented voice on the line said, "I'm going to Greece, would you like to
come to see where I was born?"

So it was arranged. We would leave our cities, meet in New York and
fly to Athens.

It had been nearly forty years since my father had seen his family.
He had started a new life in America seemingly never looking back. It
was as though he had exorcised something painful or useless from his
history. So I was surprised, when on the plane, he began to talk of what

he remembered of his childhood. The trip seemed for my father a kind of mission or pilgrimage. I assumed there was some nervousness as well. It's the same for all of us I suspect regardless of age. Going home reduces us to children. All of our achievements, experiences and futures pull us forward while our 'homes', the starting point, like the gravitational pull of a planet pulls us back to when we didn't know the world except in dreams. Odd, but I think we want to go in both directions, but finally must choose before we're torn apart. I thought my father had made his choices. I was wrong.

I do believe it's true that you can never go home again but I think it's equally true that you leave something of yourself back where you began. So it was for my father, who years before had sailed the sea to a new land. Now the past was pulling him back to where he began, back to where the secrets were kept.

After one week in Athens, my father was happy and carefree. Greece can do that. I felt it, too.

In Piraeus we booked passage for Crete. In Khania, we were met by my cousins and together we drove up to my father's village. The little town with its dirt streets and olive groves contained no more than fifty people. Almost all were relations.

From a white house with bright blue shutters, a man appeared. He was about six feet tall and slender. He had a thick gray head of hair and a long, white handlebar mustache. Also, from the house came a woman dressed in black. She was very old and small and her black form in front of the stark white house made it appear as though she had been painted on the wall by some ancient hands. Soon four people were standing outside of the small house. In my life I saw my father cry twice. The first time was when my mother died. The second was on that day.

They all stood frozen and then they were together hugging and kissing.

That night the entire village prepared food. People set up tables outside along the dirt road. They carried on until the next morning. My father's little sister, Mary, sat next to me. She kept turning and smiling and under the table she held my hand. They laughed and argued but sometimes it would get quiet and they would just look at one another trying to take it all in, remembering how each had looked those many years ago. Everything had been perfect but something was not said between them all. It was felt.

The next morning my father and I went to a cemetery. It was odd walking through a cemetery in Greece that had stones with German names. The names were those of soldiers who had fought and died here. Many dates showed that they had been young, some no more than boys. My father stepped in front of two stones. His face grew tight. The sadness was unbearable. Without a word my father betrayed his secret. After a long time he pulled a handkerchief from his pocket and looked out over the surrounding hills. Then again he looked at the stones.

"It's like a garden," he said.

But watching my father as his mind wandered through time opening the once locked doors of memory, I thought it to be a sad garden whose only harvest was regret.

A BEAUTIFUL SANDWICH

Journal entry
29 July 2004
Genova, Italy

Petite woman who looks like Audrey Hepburn walks elegantly by the 'Café des Artistes' where I am sitting. She stops, opens her tasteful handbag and pulls out the biggest sandwich (ham I think) that I have ever seen and I mean big with the meat overflowing the bread's borders. She eats with pleasure and in the corners of her wide smile there are flecks of yellow, mustard perhaps? She leaves a trail of crumbs leading to who knows where. She's beautiful. I'm hungry.

CLASS LIKE VOODOO

Journal entry
3 March 1993
London

I love England. It always feels comfortable, steady and seemingly never changing.

The British have an air of superiority but this masks a deep insecurity. The country has been psychologically damaged by the class system. Class, like voodoo, can only hurt you if you believe in it and oh how they believe in it, even when they say they don't.

ADIEU MADELEINE LEVY

Journal entry
15 November 2006
Paris

It has been a day steeped in the past, a past that is also present.

I started my day early and went to Montparnasse cemetery. The information booklet describes the person buried in section 28, number 1, as *victime réhabilitée*. It is there that the rehabilitated victim Lieutenant Colonel Alfred Dreyfus is buried.

France I'm sure does not like to be reminded of the Dreyfus affair or their past and for that matter, their present anti-Semitism. The prosecution of Dreyfus in 1894 was an exhibition of France's institutional anti-Semitism and a prelude to the deportation of 76,000 Jewish men, women and children from France to German concentration camps from 1942 to 1944.

All around the Dreyfus grave are other large tombs. Many are Jewish. I was struck by the number of stones that gave the date of the deceased's deportation from France and to where they were sent. A number of them have the names Drancy and Auschwitz. I find this part of the cemetery unsettling and I become sad, agitated and a bit angry for the pictures of my own experiences in Sierra Leone begin to leach out of the part of my brain that usually keeps them tightly contained. I can never get my head around massive and wanton murder and I confess that I want to strike out at the aggressors and return them to the dust. I am always for the victim and unlike many of my fellow liberals I have no rationalizations to offer as to why the aggressor should not be stopped or killed. I believe they should be killed. Just like today, I believe that talk with Sudan, while they engage in brutal genocide against black Africans is ridiculous and if I may, immoral. After WWII the world promised that genocide would not be allowed to happen again. Though it has failed in keeping that promise many times since, the world should keep its promise now and immediately start killing the *janjaweed* and the leaders in Khartoum if that is what it takes. I feel that is much preferable to another woman being raped or another child being murdered or a farmer having his eyes gouged out.

I suspect a family member of one of the deported dead here was very angry as well and could not contain that anger. A small sign has been placed permanently on a grave stating that the deceased had been deported by the French and murdered by the German barbarians. That sign, along with the graves, are a constant reminder of depravity and murder. It is also a cautionary tale stating emphatically that tyranny can never be negotiated or partnered with.

As I walked the narrow paths between the graves, I found myself in front of Alfred Dreyfus's grave again. I noticed the other family names on the grave. The second name caught my eye. Her name had been Madeleine Levy and she was the granddaughter of Alfred Dreyfus. I was to learn later that day (at the Mémorial de la Shoah, Musée, Centre de Documentation Juive Contemporaine) that Madeleine had been a girl scout and a social worker and although her family had been warned of increased danger, Madeleine returned to Toulouse to work and to gather belongings from her family's apartment. There, she was arrested and sent to Drancy.

In 1943 Madeleine Levy was placed on Convoy No. 62 with eighty-three children whom she cared for on the trip. She arrived at Auschwitz and in a short period of time fell ill with typhus. She died in January, 1944, and it is said that she weighed less than seventy pounds at the time of her death. I traveled to the Memorial de la Shoah in the 4th *arrondissement* and a very kind lady named Alina Dollat took out her umbrella and in the rain helped me find Madeleine Levy's name among the thousands of names on the wall of remembrance. There she was, with so many others.

I went back to Montparnasse cemetery and as I sat by the grave, I thought of my first reading of Zola's *J'Accuse* and how moved I had been, not merely because of the writing but by the courageous action of one man who took on the army and state, the Catholics and the monarchists, and risked much personally in trying to right a terrible injustice. I believe Zola thought that the court martial did not just harm Dreyfus but was a societal cancer that had the potential of destroying his beloved France. Zola, in my view, was the best kind of patriot, one that does not goosestep in line just because the state says to. I think that Zola may have also believed that some stains cannot be washed out. He and John Donne had a bit in common.

With all of this history, it still took until 1995 for President Chirac to publicly apologize for France's deportation of the Jews in WWII and to turn over to the Shoah all of the prefecture registration cards of that period that kept track of the Jews in France. Why so long? After living here for a time and myself coming from a country that also denies and fabricates its history, I think I understand. Anti-semitism is alive and well in France as it is in many places in the world. But France has only grudgingly looked at its past. Some French friends tell me that it is complicated and that the truth is hard to find. I counter that sometimes the truth is very simple and that people who do not wish to confront the truth overcomplicate events so as to claim it an unsolvable puzzle and then dismiss it. The truth is rather straightforward. Occupied France rounded up and deported thousands of its own citizens to concentration camps where the vast majority were murdered.

In Sudan the truth is quite simple as well. Men, women and children are being raped and murdered for what little they have and the color of their skin and the world is doing nothing, as it did nothing in Rwanda and Sierra Leone.

I have always believed that history is not in the past. It keeps rolling in front of us and we keep running into it. Now, we are running into history again. So, I'm not surprised when I talk to my Jewish friends in Paris and they tell me that they are always prepared to leave when things get more difficult. Some say they are scared. Others say they see familiar signs that cause them to worry and also there are the Muslims who reside in France that the government seems frightened of and all too willing to placate. The key here is that my Jewish friends are worried. For me, they are like the canary in the cage down in the mine. More sensitive to their surroundings with a history that demands vigilance.

Looking down at the map and plan of the cemetery I saw one last indignity. I realized that Alfred Dreyfus' name was incorrect. It was listed as Albert Dreyfus and had his rank as captain. France should be reminded again, and always that here lies, Lieutenant Colonel Alfred Dreyfus, Knight in the Legion of Honor

Born: October 9, 1859

Died July 12, 1935

THE FINEST CONCERT

Journal entry
22 May 2001
Florence, Italy

I get off the main street by the Piazza Della Republica and head down side streets where Italians are living their lives but clearly Florence survives by the grace or curse of tourism.

Last evening I found a restaurant named Ottorino and it was wonderful. All Italians except for me, and two strange American women who ordered veal and diet Coke while the waiters in crisp white jackets swore under their breaths.

Our waiter is Franco and thankfully he did not put us in the same camp as the loud, dieting women. He was gracious, knowledgeable and very helpful in directing us to what he thought was best. I ordered a wine and he suggested one that was cheaper. It was wonderful.

Tonight we went back to Ottorino and Franco opened a bottle of Brunello Grappa as his gift to us. Kris and I were both touched and after dinner I asked the headwaiter who spoke English to translate something for me. He called for Franco but the other waiters huddled around us as well. I said that I had the good fortune to travel around the world and taste many wonderful foods in wonderful places but that I had never been treated as well as I had been by Franco. I said that I greatly appreciated his hospitality and kindness and that I would always remember him for providing two magical nights that Kris and I would never forget. As the headwaiter translated I could see Franco's eyes tearing and when the translation was finished the other waiters applauded.

A light rain was falling as we left the restaurant and walked toward the Uffizi. In the distance we heard a violin playing Mozart. There were about 100 people who stood in the square under umbrellas listening to a young man in torn jeans playing as if in a trance. His name is Regius Ramski, so he says, and when I left it seemed that he had thousands of lire in his violin case. It was one of the finest concerts I've ever attended.

FUNDING YOUR OWN ASSASSINS

Journal entry
September 1990
Montpellier, France

This afternoon has been remarkable and unsettling. After a few days here I have asked the young Muslim woman who runs the hotel if she would allow me to take her to tea so we can talk. I want to know what it is like for a Muslim woman to live here.

She is very different from what I expect though I'm not really sure what I expected. M, I will call her, is independent, proud and efficient. She wears modern clothing and no veil. She is outgoing, funny and bright. M speaks French, Italian, Arabic, and, luckily for me, perfect English. She also possesses a very healthy strain of dark humor, which I appreciate and I think my appreciation endears me to her just a bit. M patiently listens as I ask her about her parents and boyfriend.

"Is it difficult to remain a Muslim woman and to be independent?" I ask. Does she appreciate Muslim men and so on? My inquiry went on and, I suspect, was a bit tedious, but she kept her composure and answered my questions with a candor that startled me. I liked her and in a short time I began to respect her for all she had struggled with and overcome. She was the kind of person that you would want as a friend. As I was about to ask more questions she said, "I would like to tell you something. My observations about the West."

"Yes I would be very interested in your view of this country and the West in general," I said.

"You in Europe and America are so naive. You are sometimes to me like children and at your worst arrogant children. You think that you know the world. You not only do not know the world you make no effort to understand it even when you are threatened."

"What do you mean threatened?" I said.

"I came to France from Morocco where I had no chances like I have here. I did not wish to be a covered woman or someone's wife. I had dreams of education and my own business. I dreamed of a life where I was equal and where I could try and experience many things."

"But this is not a perfect place," I replied. "There is much prejudice here as there is in my country. Is that not a problem for you?"

"There is prejudice everywhere. My white French boyfriend of two years is still afraid to introduce me to his parents."

"That must make you angry."

"It frustrates me but it does not make me angry. I still have my independence and my dreams and I am in a place where some of them may come true and are coming true. But people like you do not understand the threat."

"That's the second time you've said threat. What do you mean threat?" I repeated.

"You should be only letting people into your countries who are like me. People who want a new life, people who have dreams and want to be part of a free society. Instead you are allowing people into the countries who disrespect your way of life, have no respect for women or your laws, hate your religion and homosexuals and hope and work for your downfall. That is not very intelligent, is it?"

"Don't you think that is a bit extreme?" I replied.

"You do not know extreme. In the West you feel that you must be equal and kind to everyone though in practice that is just words. You want to feel righteous. But when you let those kinds of people in, they do not move in next to you, they live next to me and they try to reduce me to what they believe a woman's or man's place should be. You are not subject to the tyranny of these people, to their ignorance and hatred but I am. But whether you see it or not, it is only a matter of time before the confined disease spreads. You are all so foolish. You are funding your own assassins."

I RISE TO THE NEWS OF WAR

Journal entry
20 March 2003
Paris

Well, it's war then.

I rise to the news that the U.S. bombing of Iraq has begun.

The ignorant bastards in Washington (with the help of the media and the American people) have now condemned Americans and others to years of violence and terrorism. Americans who support this authoritarian action and regime think that this will be over quickly. They are wrong. Democrats who betrayed principal on an altar of re-election hope should be ashamed. It was their job to ask hard questions. They failed miserably. I can see a future Democratic candidate who voted for the war one day campaign, when the war is going badly of course, against the president and his party for getting us into the war and the public will buy it. The press will go after (too late) those who made bold promises and try to cover up their (the press') own culpability.

What all sides have in common is hypocrisy and that hypocrisy will now have a cost in lives. Do the public or press or politicians not study any history at all? Have they read *A Peace to End All Peace* or the chapter, 'Semitic Religiosity' in T. E. Lawrence's *Seven Pillars of Wisdom?* Hubris and ignorance have a cost.

The facts are these: thousands of Ottoman soldiers could not find and kill Lawrence and his band of insurgents in the Hajaz during WW I. If we (the US) do not get this stabilized in the first 180 days, we will not get it at all and then we will be like the Ottoman Turks. An insurgency WILL take place, foreigners maybe, locals, for sure. They will be like mosquitoes that bite, disappear and bite again. We will lose soldiers every day and kill thousands of innocent and not so innocent civilians. We will torture people in interrogations like the French in Algeria. A civil war will follow and then we will leave.

I stood on the *Pont des Arts* and watched as the boats passed.
A Frenchman standing a few paces away asked,
"*Americain?*"
"*Oui,*" I replied. "American."
"*Désolé,*" he said as he offered me a drink of wine from his plastic glass. I said thank you and there we stood not saying another word.

I looked at the sky hanging above *Ile de la Cité*. It showed no evidence of the storm that I felt was coming.

(Note) Upon reviewing this journal entry for the volume I was struck by its tone which, suggested prescience, insight or special wisdom. It was nothing of the sort. I had simply read many excellent books concerning history over the years such as David Fromkin's A Peace to End All Peace or Seven Pillars of Wisdom (T.E. Lawrence) The Koran (Oxford translation), Among the Believers (V.S. Naipaul) and, biographies about Sir Richard Francis Burton, Gertrude Bell and Winston Churchill. I had also read much concerning Ibn Saud and the 18th century Muslim sect started by Muhammad Ibn Al-Wahhab. After understanding the colonial powers' past motivations, true intent, miscalculations and failures, it was not hard to conclude that the United States was making similar errors in judgment. Prior to the current conflict the last British occupation of Iraq was during WWII from 1939-45. Like the American's statements at the beginning of the current war in Iraq, the British, too, thought that their occupation would last only a 'few months' but after the monarchy was restored they remained until the late 1950's and left during the revolution. Following the British departure, and after a number of military coups, Saddam Hussein took power in 1968.

After considering these facts it was neither difficult, nor prescient, to conclude that the United States and others in the 'coalition of the willing' were ill prepared intellectually to understand or communicate effectively with the Iraqi population. Also, as was increasingly apparent in the beginnings of the conflict, the United States was unprepared militarily and psychologically to fight a guerrilla war. The invasion was based on a false premise. I came to that conclusion in the weeks leading up to the war because the U.S. government had stated many numbers of times that they had 'proof' Iraq had weapons of mass destruction but never provided any solid evidence to support their claims. I was reminded of the Tonkin Gulf fiction that escalated our involvement in Vietnam. It all had an odor of something familiar. At the time of this writing, a new Congress has been elected with Democrats in the majority. The war in Iraq is in shambles and there is ongoing and increasing sectarian violence that many are reluctant to call a civil war but is. President Bush is now asking for an additional 20,000 troops and more funds for the war.

One year after the Iraqi war began I was reminded of a letter written by T.E. Lawrence to the Sunday Times on 22 August 1920.

Lawrence writes:

"The people of England have been led in Mesopotamia into a trap from which it will be hard to escape with dignity and honour. They have been tricked into it by a steady withholding of information. The Bagdad communiqués are belated, insincere, incomplete. Things have been far worse than we have been told, our administration more bloody and inefficient than the public knows. It is a disgrace to our imperial record, and may soon be too inflamed for an ordinary cure. We are to-day not far from a disaster."

I DO NOT LIKE TEXAS

Letter
George Katakis, Chicago, Illinois
August 1974
Dallas, Texas

Dear Papa,

I must say I do not like Texas. It is 'vulgar'. What a strange word for a mid-western boy, maybe the word is cruel or selfish. I think of Kennedy as I look up at the window where it is said, and I don't believe, the assassin took aim and killed not just the man but a whole lot of dreams. This place seems like the right place to kill a dream, hopeless. The poor here are polite and dominated while the rich are, well, vulgar. The women wear lots of paint on their faces and really like to talk loud and show off their jewelry, often in front of folks with little. Really strange, and unkind. The only thing I know is if the country puts one of these jokers in the White House again we are really in trouble which will mean that the country has become pretty vulgar itself.

A STOMACH FULL OF GRAPPA

Journal entry
11 January 2007
Carmel, California

Early this morning I went on my ocean walk. It was dark when I set out with the exception of a bit of light from a half moon. Walking along the beach I heard a grunting sound and then escaping air. I realized that not far from shore a whale was clearing his blowhole. I laughed with joy and was reminded of Italy a few years ago when at one or two in the morning under a full moon and a stomach full of grappa, I stripped and floated on the Ligurian sea and stared at the moon and stars above me and then turned to see their reflections dancing around me. While floating, memories of responsibilities imposed themselves and I was reminded of promises to keep. I drifted again and realized that the moon and stars and sea knew me for what I am, a transient thing, short lived, a memory of wished and unrealized dreams. I was of no consequence there and it gave me peace for unimportance has its place. It felt that way again this morning, alone, in the dark, with the sounds of the ocean.

I HOPE SHE MADE IT TO PARIS

Journal entry
4 October 2006
Paris

I walked through the Jardin de Luxembourg this afternoon. It was cool and many people were bundled in their wool coats and scarves. Couples and children everywhere.

The small ponies moved back and forth over the dry leaves that crunched under their hooves as their little riders giggled or cried or stroked the sides of their necks. Many chairs were empty and throughout the park they were left as singles, pairs or groups leaving suggestions of who had been there. The two chairs close together suggested lovers and the ones bunched up by the pond spoke of families watching excited children pushing sailboats. The chairs were telling their recent histories everywhere. Amid a large group of empty chairs, I saw an older couple kissing and fondling each other.

As I watched them from a distance, I was reminded of a story that a friend had told me in the United States. He had been at a restaurant and had overheard a conversation between an elderly woman and a young man. The older woman said, "Do you have any idea how it feels to know that you will never be touched that way again, I mean with passion and desire? To never again know and feel that is almost unbearable."

I was deeply moved when I first heard that story and it has always stayed with me and made me a little sad. As I watched the old couple kissing, I wished that I could find that woman and tell her to come to Paris. There is touching here, with hands and eyes and smells. You do not see what is lost here. In Paris romance is not only for the young but also for the living, for anyone who desires. Leaving the garden I watched as an older woman with high heels and shapely legs watched me watching her. As she passed me, her gait slowed and there was a hint of a smile and, a momentary scent of lavender. I looked back at the elderly woman with beautiful legs and hoped that the woman, who my friend had overheard, made it to Paris.

Journal Entry
20 September 2004
England, The River Ouse (Walking the South Downs Way, approx: 100 miles)

It's a cool, rainy day and I am seemingly in the middle of nowhere like a man who finds himself transported through space and time in a Twilight Zone episode. I am standing next to the River Ouse and there is a melancholy that washes over me.

The River Ouse, oh yes I remember now. In 1941 Virginia Woolf ended her life here. Was it a day like today I wonder. Did she feel the melancholy, too, or was she at peace while picking up the rocks that would help her descend below the slow moving water? Where did she enter? Was it close to where I am standing?

Did the location matter at all or was it the entire river that first whispered, enticed and finally, welcomed her below to drift and remember and inhale. Did she still think that, "…madness is terrific?"

In one's own depression things are magnified. Small pains, exhaustion, a desire to end, but other people's pains are magnified as well as if to create invisible comrades. To not be alone with the 'black dog' and to seek some shred of hope and relief from the possibility that this may be your life, always. That hope, while necessary, is precarious and fragile and sometimes itself too heavy and one just lets go. I suspect letting go gave Virginia some peace. A decision was made at last that ensured the pain was not infinite and that she herself had some control.

The air is filled with moisture but the rain has stopped and in the distance I thought I heard a train. I love trains.

Not today Virginia.

SOMEWHERE IN CHINA / I AM LOST

Journal Entry
July 1984
China

I have been wandering around China and have landed in this small village. I think it is may be a hundred miles north of Guillin but I'm not sure. I left my map somewhere a few days ago (stupid) and have been winging it ever since. My Chinese, non-existent, and so far I have met no one and I mean no one who speaks English. I wonder how Marco Polo did it.

It is late in the evening here but the little main street (if I can call it that) is still alive with some assorted food carts. Earlier today I came by and saw this young boy selling melons. He had a mountain of them. That mountain is considerably smaller now and the boy appears to be tallying his day's earnings. I have tried to photograph it and hope it has come out. He has a kerosene lamp and it throws off a very bright light. The boy, with pencil in hand, is a study in concentration. As I have traveled through China, one thing is always apparent and that is how hard the Chinese work. In the many rice fields I have crossed, I have never seen any machinery for farming. I have only witnessed ox and man. Can they really be feeding over a billion people this way with maybe some foreign food subsidies? If these people had more education and opportunity, I would not like to compete against them. They are amazing and have been very kind to me. Today I set up the camera in a rice field to take a self-portrait with a young Chinese farmer who was showing me how to plant rice. This kind young man and his family laughed as, repeatedly, my planting was not up to standard. I think I became the afternoon's entertainment. These lovely people fed me and offered me their bed. I could not keep up with their work ethic and I don't believe many in America could either. Their burden for the future, however, is the number of people.

STILL LOST IN CHINA

Journal entry
July 1984
China

I am still lost somewhere in the countryside and my frustration is added to by the fact that I am not really present. My mind keeps going back to the young woman I met. Her name is Kris. She is an anthropologist who has lived for years in Sierra Leone, West Africa, and now is at the Smithsonian. She is someone very special and I can't get her out of my mind. I wish I were not here or could get her out of my head. What is strange is that, for the first time a woman has lingered on my mind. I must confess, however, that I like the thought of her here with me if only in memory. I want to cut my trip short and go to Washington to see her. How ridiculously romantic.

Journal entry
10 June 1988
Kainkordu, West Africa

In Sierra Leone, among the Kuranko people, it is believed that some human beings are able to transform themselves into animals or things. These people are known as *Yelamanfentiginu,* 'change thing masters'. They are almost always men. Witches are nearly always women. Both can bring death.

Now, standing here alone I am trying to understand what has happened to me. I want to get it down before I rationalize it away, before the fear is dismissed as irrational.

In London, on the night before my flight to West Africa, I had a dream. I dreamt that I was drowning in elephant grass. I jumped, trying to see over the top but the grass grew higher. I ran and the thin blades cut my face and arms. I stood bleeding and exhausted, surrounded by elephant grass that continued to grow. Before me, a black man appeared. His features were soft. He smiled but it was a wicked smile. I wondered why he was smiling seeing that he, too, was trapped. His smile then disappeared and he turned into a small bird. The bird flew high above me as the grass continued to grow, slowly blocking out the light of the moon. Just before the grass closed completely around me, a satellite drifted past the small opening. I woke suddenly. The sheets were soaked.

I don't believe in premonitions of fate. I believe, or I should say I believed, that I controlled my own destiny. At that moment in the hotel, I had a vested interest in preserving that illusion. I did not want my new bride to think her worldly husband was shaken by some absurd dream. But I was shaken. It was the smell. It was the first time I had ever smelled something in a dream and even after I woke I could still detect that musty odor but could not place it with anything in the room.

We hurried to the airport gate and the line of people rushing to board with their exotic features and brilliantly colored clothing were in sharp contrast to the calm of the airport. We settled into our seats. My wife was already asleep when the steward placed a blanket over her and asked if I'd like a drink. As I drifted toward sleep, I thought of Sigmund Freud.

Freud believed that repression was forgetting and forgetting that you'd forgotten. I rationalized that my dream had nothing to do with some strange external force trying to warn me, but rather was myself trying to exorcise some dark secret from some forgotten past. Freud might have interpreted the grass closing around me as loss of freedom due to marriage. The bird overhead might also symbolize freedom now out of reach. Thus, with makeshift psychology, I dismissed my dream as easily as Scrooge dismissed Marley's ghost. It was nothing more than a bit of indigestion. My western logic did not make allowances for superstition or premonitions or magic. I put the dream out of my mind secure that I could conquer any personal demons, or at least ignore them. I was wrong.

A voice preparing us for landing awakened me and my wife was surprised to find that I was covered in sweat. A raw fear was taking hold and as it washed over me I wanted to scream or jump up, anything. I closed my eyes took deep breaths and grabbed the armrests so tightly that my hands cramped. The plane taxied and stopped and I became calm as the plane's doors opened and the hot, thick, humid air rushed in.

The next morning after checking in at the U.S. Embassy in Freetown we began our trip 200 miles east to Kainkordu. That first night in Koidu, I dreamt again of elephant grass. This time there were people with lights and they were sobbing. The lights disappeared into the tall grass and then it was silent and dark. I woke to the musty smell that I had experienced in London. I began to consider the possibility that I was losing my mind.

After three days in Koidu we secured transport for the twenty-mile journey to Kainkordu. Tin and thatched roofs appeared as we topped the last hill before entering Kainkordu. People rushed the vehicle to see who had come. Immediately they recognized Kris. Kris, an anthropologist, had lived in this village for two years. There was much greeting and soon we were surrounded by what seemed the entire town. The Kono took Kris returning with her new husband as a great honor and after more greetings the paramount chief selected a house to be our home for the next two months. Sahr, a young man from the village became our guide, interpreter and friend.

The bad day began at 10:00 a.m. A woman who lived near us became very ill and at first it was thought to be malaria but soon everyone realized it was something much worse. At 1:20 p.m. the woman went into convulsions. At 2:45 p.m. she died. Some villagers believed that she had been possessed. The dead woman's daughter then fell ill and by 4:00 p.m. she, too, was dead. Witchcraft was now being whispered about. By 5:40 p.m. the sister of the dead girl was also dying in a fit of horrible convulsions and the village began to panic. Kris was called and she, like everyone else, tried desperately to piece together the events and find a rational explanation for what was happening. While Kris was asking more questions, two more people died. All of the dead were from the same family. As the panic grew more intense, a villager discovered a link. All the dead had washed their hair that day and all had shared the same cleanser. What had been thought to be a de-licer was in fact an extremely toxic defoliant. It wasn't witchcraft at all, it was just a horrible mistake but many villagers believed it had been witch's work and names were being mentioned.

By 10:20 p.m. five people were dead, two were very ill and a seven-year-old girl was struggling to live. Watching with everyone else, I stood in the night surrounded by elephant grass, as kerosene lanterns were held high to light the scene. There was a small fire that gave off a familiar musty odor. A little girl was lying in the lap of a man who was placing a tube down her throat. She did not struggle and then she was still. Family and friends wept as the lamplights divided in different directions and then disappeared into the night's blackness. I stood there looking at the little girl. The man who had tried to help her turned and stared at me and in the dim firelight I saw his face. It was the face in my dream. He was smiling but it was a wicked smile. I turned away and a blade of elephant grass cut my cheek and it began to bleed. From behind me there was a rustling noise. I turned again to see that face and the girl's lifeless body. The man was gone.

I walked back to the house and stared at the wide and clear African sky. No satellites. Even premonitions can be mistaken I thought. I don't recall my dream that night.

Journal entry
7 November 2006
Paris

Passage d'Enfer explodes with a sound like a marching band. I jump out of bed, open the apartment window wide and the cold November air rushes in. Below my window, on the old uneven cobblestones stands a giant of a man with a broad smile bundled up in winter clothing cranking his harmonium.

"*Bonjour*" he yells as he sees me. He then throws me a big kiss.

"*Bonjour Monsieur, ça va?*"

"*Oui*" I yell back. "*Je vais bien. Et vous?*"

"*Très bien, merci,*" he shouts back.

It's like I'm a kid again and the circus has come to town or I'm in a Marcello Mastroianni movie. The happy, goofy, cheerful music is bouncing off the buildings and people are opening their doors and windows. Smiles everywhere and everyone ignoring the cold. I grab a two Euro coin and throw it down to his assistant who unfortunately, is a woman, rather than a monkey, which I had envisioned and hoped for. She catches the coin in a small wicker basket and the big guy yells,

"*Merci monsieur.*" I yell back "*Merci beaucoup.*"

He moves on down the passage over the old cobblestones cranking out the grand, ridiculous, glorious, music until he disappears down Blvd. Raspail.

What a way to start the day. *Merci, monsieur. Merci.*

Journal entry
9 October 2006 Month of Ramadan
Fez, Morocco

On the ferry we passed the promontories at the eastern end of the Strait of Gibraltar which are the Pillars of Hercules. There is the Rock of Gibraltar (Europe) and Jebel Musa (Ceuta) in North Africa. The fable is that the promontories were set there by Heracles as a memorial for his seizing the cattle that belonged to the three-bodied Geryon.

As we pressed on we saw the land that is Northern Africa. Wonderful and good to be back somewhere in Africa. In Tangier we went straight to the train for Fez.

On the train I met a remarkable, young (20 years old) Muslim woman named Fatima. Fatima is dressed like a Parisian woman with a fashionable dress and high heels. I see that she has received some very disparaging looks on the train from other partly covered women. She wears a wedding ring but is not married. She does so, so men will leave her alone. She is working on a Ph.D. in tourism, whatever that means, and already speaks four languages. She spent two hours telling Kris and me what it is like being a woman in Morocco. She then asks what religion I am. I say I am agnostic. She leans across Kris and says that she is sorry that we do not have more time together for she would show me what God is. I must say I was intrigued. Fatima is a modern, young, Muslim woman full of contradictions and beautiful dreams. I wish her well.

Fez is interesting but at times not so enjoyable. It is somewhat trapped into a tour bus mentality. A construct of sorts. I wandered the Medina and watched as tourists were hustled here and there with winks and nods being exchanged by the guides as well as cash. I hired a guide for a few hours, Ali. He was finally good when he realized I was not interested in trinkets or carpets. He then got serious and took us to some remarkable places like the Jewish cemetery. He said he found us unusual because "everyone wants to buy things," and no one seems interested in the history of Fez beyond taking photographs to show they were here. It is important to realize however that no matter how much you believe you are making a connection with people here you are not. There is a layering of life here that does not wish to change but does want tourism. They see us, I think, a bit like an infection or bacteria that they are trying hard to figure out how to live with without succumbing to. I believe, like everywhere, if they are not careful they will compromise themselves. Oddly however, in this case, I believe that compromise might be beneficial and help them move beyond pronounced contradictions.

Being in Morocco at Ramadan has been interesting and at times funny. I resisted taking many taxis because it appears that there are more accidents at Ramadan because the drivers fall asleep behind the wheel more frequently. I love the late night here after evening prayers. I wander the back streets and just fall in with the rhythm of the place. In all of the cafes, men, men and more men. No women. I will never get used to that. Kris reminded me that many marriages are arranged here and that the women, who may or may not have anything in common with their husbands, may really enjoy the separation from the men.

One thing is painfully clear. There is a similarity that is happening in many places like Fez or Athens or cities in Italy. Tourists are dragged to pre-prescribed places and they are shown and told that for a moment, in history, these societies once possessed greatness which conversely magnifies how far they have fallen into tour bus tourism that has reduced their people into low paid servants and hustlers. The new colonialism is global and predatory and alive and well. It offers a precarious future.

ANZAC COVE

Journal entry
25 September 2005
Gallipoli

Today I went to one of the most beautiful places I have ever seen – odd that not so long ago it was a place of hubris and death. Worlds collided here and names like Churchill and Mustafa Kemal weaves in and out of that history.

Anzac Cove is stunning with its sad beach and blue green sea. It is absent of any signs or hawkers but there is a subtle and dignified monument which explains some of what went on here from the perspective of both sides. It is disarmingly calm. Looking up at the surrounding hills that in 1914-16 rained down munitions, it seems incredible that the military continued to sacrifice good men in such unsuitable fighting conditions.

Kris and I took a detour and swam in the gin clear, cold Aegean. In the distance was Imroz I think.

A SENSE OF FOREBODING

Letter
DeWitt Sage, Greenwich, CT
4 July 2004
Rapallo, Italy

Dear DeWitt,
As to my living and traveling throughout Europe, I have experienced a sense of foreboding somewhat like a faint scent momentarily experienced and then gone. My impression is coming from a variety of sources. There are conversations and looks given to certain people as they pass, body language, whispers and an apparent growing frustration and anger. The words often used in response to my questions are assimilation, immigration, terror, work, religion, Muslim and America.

Being the son of an immigrant, I am well aware of the implied contract that has existed between immigrant and state. Simply put, the immigrant agreed to assimilate, obey the laws of the country and respect, if not appreciate, the culture. The state was obliged to provide work and opportunity and maintain order so as to create a stable environment where the immigrants could elevate themselves and, perhaps prosper. It is clear that this implied agreement is coming under increased pressure from both sides.

I have talked with many Muslim men and women from Bozeman, Montana, New York, Paris, London and Montpellier, France among others. In my conversations it is clear that many Muslim men, of a certain age, have a problem with the idea of assimilation or disregard it altogether. Muslim women less so if they are not under pressure, which I have found they often are. Sharia law has been mentioned more than a few times which, of course, is totalitarianism by another name and completely incompatible with a free society. You want to know about Sharia? Read Orwell's Animal Farm and you've got it. The observations of Naipaul and Rushdie have currency here in explaining the Arab and Islamic contradictions and Edward Said's views give a balanced counter. I always remind myself that my country, as well as others, allowed many people to immigrate because of the supposed need for cheap labor but now, thanks to the blight of globalization, corporations are taking jobs anywhere where there are even poorer and more desperate people to exploit. The state and corporations (Plutocracy) have clearly broken their implied contract, as have some Muslims and others who are not assimilating and respecting the culture they now find themselves in. There is pressure, it is mounting and as opportunities narrow, more and more people are in the streets.

I have heard it said that the world is becoming more dangerous for non-Muslims but I think the reverse to be true. I have encountered hate speech that I suspect is not very different from the vitriol that was directed at the Jews prior to WWII.

Do I think there is a threat? Well, I cannot discount the realities of Spain, New York, Bali and Africa to name a few, but with that said, I believe that it is terribly important at this time in our history for societies to keep their heads and not overreact or play into extremist's (theirs or our) hands.

The irony now is that many of the world's leaders seem to have something in common with the Bin Ladens of the world. They can tear things down but seem incapable of building anything up. Blair, who I once respected, wanted to be Churchill but it is not a Churchillian time. Bush wanted to be baseball commissioner.

Propagandists always deal in generalizations and partial truths and I'm sorry to say are often successful in their manipulations. Unfortunately for them I have met people like Abdul, in Italy, who is trying hard to have a life. His command of languages is impressive, certainly better than mine, and he is a fine cook who works very hard and makes the best pasta with clams that I have ever had. He takes great pride in that, as he should. Then there is Midi in Paris who loves books and wants to be an intellectual who argues ideas well. He is trying to find his way and make a life that is not at the expense of others. Contrary to the propagandists on all sides, I will never be convinced, that people like Midi and Abdul are not the Muslim majority. However, I will feel that something has changed dramatically and positively when Muslim men march in the streets of Paris for the right of Muslim women everywhere to take OFF the veil...

SECULAR? GOOD MUSLIM, BAD MUSLIM

Letter
Harold Gurnee, Sharon, CT
1 October 2005
Istanbul

Dear Hal,
Well it has been a remarkable few weeks. At present I am enjoying a very cold Efes pilsner on the Sea of Marmara. Earlier today I was on the Bosporus. Behind me lay Europe, ahead Asia, and the river dividing the two a metaphor for this extraordinary country.

Turkey is fascinating and while I have covered much ground I have only scratched the surface. The Turkish people have been exceedingly kind but the Turks do have an internal struggle. At times it seems as if they are trying to determine how to define themselves. Secular? Good Muslim, bad Muslim. Modern civilization or an older path to some supposed piety. Fundamentalism or Ataturk's wish to see "all religions at the bottom of the sea." One can feel the teetering between two worlds. The delicate balancing act contributes to the appeal of the place.

Boarded the ferry at Eminou and traveled up the Bosporus to the last stop on the Asia side, Anadolu Kavagi.

Kris and I hiked up to the 14th century Byzantine fortress 'Genoese Castle' and looked out across the straits into the Black Sea. Magic. Worked up a good appetite and had some Imam Bayeldi (the Imam fainted). Eggplant with onion, garlic and olive oil. Fantastic with a cold beer and bread. Returning on the river there were jellyfish everywhere and a light rain. On arrival boarded another ferry to the Asia side and the train station at Haydarpasa. It was like being transported back to 1914 and I loved it. The ticket collector asked me politely if Bush was a racist. I said no, he dislikes everyone equally unless you have a great deal of money. The man laughed and said Turkey had a few like that, too. The next morning I drove to Gallipoli (5 hours). First I went to the Royal Navy Battleship memorial and looked out across the Dardanelles. Thousands died here. There is a strange and quiet beauty that combined with a powerful silence feels as if it will endure the ages. It is a place where all of the promise and hopes of those lost waits. Just waits.

The food here is just wonderful, stuffed peppers and grape leaves. There are eggplant dishes that are so good it is hard to believe. I have become (like Ataturk) addicted to Raki and the mezzes (little bites) that are served with it, delicious, delicious!

Best,

Michael

ART THAT IS ALIVE

Letter
Michael Palin, London, England
19 October 2006
Madrid, Spain

Dear Michael,

I am now in Madrid for a few days after a fine trip to Morocco. Much learned and much more to understand. I leave for Paris (In shaa Allah) in a few days and will very much appreciate some rest.

I went to the Museo' Nacional Centro de Arte Reina Sofia. There were wonderful paintings by Juan Gris and a number of artists I had not seen before. I saw *Guernica* for the first time and must confess that it is not a great painting but rather a very powerful statement and strangely current. The paintings that really surprised and have now stayed with me are by an artist I never cared for, or I thought I did not care for until now. Salvador Dali's 'The Enigma of Hitler 1938-39' and 'Atomic Melancholia 1944-45' still haunt me. He was prescient and the paintings are foreboding and dangerous. This is art that was and is alive. It transcends time and place. It is for me reminiscent of when, as a young fellow of eighteen, I saw Van Gogh's self-portrait. You know the one with the bandage around his head covering the self-inflicted wound. The old story goes that he cut off his ear as a presentation to someone he was infatuated with. When I first saw that painting at the end of a narrow hall, I knew very little about Van Gogh and his life but that painting really scared me. The hair on the back of my neck stood up and while I wanted to turn away, I moved closer to it and as I did, I got lost in his eyes and the eyes held me for what seemed a long time and scared me even more. Later, as I learned more about his life, I realized that he had painted madness and I had reason to be scared. Years later when I had my own episode it was a feeling much like that fear in that museum many years before and I dreamt of his eyes.

For me art is when it shakes your foundations and preconceptions, when it takes you to places you never thought of going to nor would have chosen.

THE SOLDIER AND THE MILKSHAKE

Letter
George Katakis, Chicago, Illinois
3 May 1982
Seoul, Korea

Dear Papa,
I walked past a fence last night that had a Chinese bike chained to it. As I walked out this morning, the frame was still chained to the fence but the back tire, seat, chain, handlebars and one pedal were gone. What strange thieves they have here. I guess the owner is going to have a bad day today.

I find Korea interesting and the people exotic and mysterious. I guess a lot of the mystery comes from not understanding the language. I'm not very good with language and I am sorry about that because it is very important to know. I also think it is more polite to have some words and to try when you are in another country. I am learning that there is a big difference between being a tourist and a traveler.

I have made the acquaintance of a South Korean soldier here. He speaks some English and he is showing me parts of Seoul and educating

me in regard to Korean culture and customs. As a thank you I took him to an American joint for a hamburger and a milkshake. I was surprised to learn that he had never had a milkshake. The soldiers here don't make the kind of money that the American soldiers do and it creates some tension. Anyway I ordered him a chocolate milkshake with a hamburger and fries. He drank a mouthful of milkshake and his eyes bugged out and he smiled and then just broke out laughing. He fell in love with milkshakes and I mean milkshakes because he downed two in very short order. He is a nice guy with a good heart. As a soldier I cannot say.

A SAD FAMILY ALBUM

Journal entry
20 August 2000
Paris (Written while preparing for the exhibition 'A Time and Place Before War' which opened in London at the Royal Geographical Society.)

One of my fondest memories of Kainkordu is waking on a bright Sunday morning and finding my friend and protector Sahr washing his three goats with an expression not unlike that of a California kid washing his new used convertible. There are many memories of that place and time that I have wanted to keep safe, but that is no longer possible.

As I look at these photographs now, they have become for me a sad family album with stories of murder, rape, and the mutilation of children and at the heart of it, diamonds.

I know in all probability that my friend Sahr was killed, along with many others in these photographs, and that Kainkordu may no longer exist. As more information emerges about what has happened in Kainkordu, my denial has turned to anger; anger at exploitative corporations and governments that facilitate unethical business in places like Sierra Leone. Above all, I am angry at the indifference of consumers around the world.

The smuggling, selling and purchasing of diamonds continues to facilitate misery and death in Sierra Leone. When I try to explain the reality of this situation, I assume others will be equally concerned. Instead, what I often find is a litany of rationalizations. Some have told me that, after all, they are only one person what could they do and what difference would it make? Others have even said "Those people (meaning Africans) are always killing each other, even before there were diamonds." I suppose in this time of selective morality it is much easier to make speeches about social justice than to apply it in our personal lives. This indifference is not my country's alone. It is a global indifference, as was recently witnessed in Rwanda.

I no longer believe in countries, corporations, nationalism or unbridled capitalism. What I believe in is the right of the people in these photographs to have lived their lives full measure, with hope that one day life could be better for themselves and their children.

Sometimes, I dream of Sahr. He is walking ahead of me quickly. From time to time he turns, smiles and motions me to catch up. In front of him, is the giant spreading tree we often passed together. I try to keep up but am always behind. Finally, I am standing alone. I can no longer look at diamonds without seeing blood on them.

ABOVE IT ALL

Journal entry
2 May 1998
Havana, Cuba

I walked past the dark opening quickly and just caught a glimpse of the great fish on the floor. I turned around and stepped into the doorway. Two old men were standing over the marlin which had just been cleaned. The man who caught the fish seemed in his late seventies and was in remarkable shape. He wore thick glasses and a Chicago Bulls' baseball cap. In my very poor Spanish I was able to learn that this man had caught the fish on a hand line and then he showed me his simple gear and where the hook was bent. He took me outside and began to show me how to cast the line from the wooden spool. His smile and enthusiasm were infectious. I told him he seemed in fantastic shape and he laughed and pulled up his shirt and there was a hard washboard stomach that any health nut at Gold's gym would envy. For a moment I just stared at this joyful old man as he went on. I realized he was above all the politics and embargos, above Fidel and America, above the chaotic lives so many of us live. Here he was living in the moment. I suspect he had always lived in the moment. He again demonstrated how to cast the line and when I finally got it right he grabbed my arm and patted my back.

"Practice." He said in Spanish, "Practice. The pleasure is in the doing you know."

Journal entry
Fall 1989
Philadelphia (University of Pennsylvania)

Kris has just finished a talk to some university faculty and alumni about her research in Africa using a number of my photographs as illustrations. After the presentation the audience gathers around the room, and the bar, discussing what has been said or, as I overhear, something about interest rates and how the 'market is doing.' I stand in the corner with drink in hand looking at Kris and am overcome with pride. How did I come to be with such a beautiful and brilliant woman I wonder? Even with this sense of pride, I look forward to the end of the evening.

A woman approaches me and introduces herself as Mrs. So and so of the so and so's of Philadelphia. She is wearing a tasteful black dress with a string of pearls and a great deal of makeup. She has thick gray hair cut short and an air of privilege and her heavy sweet perfume nearly makes me ill. She is slurring some of her words and it is clear that what she is drinking is not her first drink of the evening.

"So you are the photographer." She says as she gestures with her drink hand.

"Yes, I am."

"Did you like Africa?"

"Yes. It is a complicated place but I found the people kind in spite of very difficult conditions."

"Yes, yes. I went to Africa once on safari. It was very dusty and the people, the blacks I mean, didn't seem to be very ambitious. Well I suppose that everyone can't be ambitious but still, you know what I mean."

"Yes," I said. "I think I understand."

"Tell me," she said in a conspiratorial hush, "how was it living among the savages?"

"Do you mean in Philadelphia?" I responded. She looked at me with shock,

"No, no I mean in Africa."

"Oh Madame, I found no savages in Africa."

LIKE EATING FOR THE FIRST TIME

Journal entry
10 June 1988
Lake Como, Italy

This morning Mr. Celli loaned me his wonderfully kept wooden boat and I rowed across Lake Como. There was a light wind that made the rowing back difficult but the lake and surrounding hills made the effort worthwhile. There always seems to be a scent of verbena in the air. Kris is at a conference at Villa Serbelloni for two weeks and I am enjoying the solitude. The little hotel where I am staying is cheap but the food is expensive and it should be. I have never tasted anything like it. The old woman prepares these small fishes with a green sauce that she will not tell me about. Its aroma and color are fantastic. I smell some parsley and basil but cannot make out the rest. All I know is that it is so fantastic that I have had it five nights in a row and if I could have it for lunch, I would. The produce is so fresh it is like eating a tomato or zucchini for the first time. At this rate my money for Africa will be gone by week's end. I feel like an addict and the old, Italian woman my dealer.

MY KIND OF COP

Journal entry
5 October 1986
Paris

There is some kind of demonstration in front of a post office. It may be a strike for it seems as though the people gathered are connected to the post office. There is a line of police officers in front of the building and they are not letting anyone in. The strikers are right up close to the police and they are yelling. I ask a policeman what is happening and he says "*manifestation*" or strike. The police have a kind of helmet on and are standing close together creating a human wall. To one side, however, I see a policeman dressed in riot gear. He has separated himself from his comrades and is looking at the menu posted on the window of a neighborhood brasserie. This is my kind of cop. It would appear that his priorities are very much in line with his culture.

After seeing him I knew it would be all right and sure enough at 1:00 p.m. nearly everyone broke for lunch.

THE LITTLE GIRL I COULD NOT SAVE

Journal entry
3 August 1988
Sierra Leone, West Africa: Kainkordu

I know now as I watch her playing that she will haunt me for the rest of my life and remind me of my impotence and powerlessness and failure. I have been watching my little neighbor for nearly a month now. She is a pretty little girl with an easy smile, pigtails and mischievous eyes. She is like little children everywhere with the exception that she is slowly dying of tuberculosis. The family has been told not to share utensils or bowls and to keep the other children from getting too close but it has not made a difference. Why would it, we are just outsiders. She is laughing this afternoon and somehow that has made me sadder because I want to extend her childish laughter into her teens and then young adulthood. I have talked with Kris a number of times about her and Kris has set me straight as to what I'm up against. I have money in my pocket that I am more than happy to just turn over but I have come to realize that money alone will not save the little girl with pigtails and sparkling eyes who is at present making faces at me and then smiles. Her teeth are so white. Someone with teeth so white can't be sick.

The treatment for tuberculosis here would take about six months. How the hell hard could that be? But I find that the little girl will have to travel a day's journey away and stay in the town for the duration of treatment. The family would need to have a connection with another family member in that place who would put her up and feed her and make sure that she got the treatments. The family would have to help pay for that. No problem, I could cover that. Then I am asked to whom I would give the money. I say the family. Then I am asked what I think the family will do with the money. They will help the girl I answer. The answer is they will not. The family must stay and tend to their crops or all of the family will find themselves short of rice and that could start to endanger them all. Furthermore, it is discovered that the family has no relations in the places where treatment is available. I'm asked about transport and I realize I have been here for a month and have seen only two vehicles pass. Finally, I realize that the parents would take the money and use it for all of their children but not for one child alone.

It is now clear that the only way I can do this is if I stay for six months or longer and do it myself. I'm not allowed to stay in the country that long and even if I could, would I? Would the parents let me take the girl for treatment? Kris talks to them and the family discusses this among themselves. They came back and said that they would give us the girl. That was the only solution they saw. She would then be Kris' and my responsibility. I could see that the mother was very pained about her little girl but she and her husband were not prepared to take money under false pretenses. They may have been poor but they were not without honor. The reality slowly dawned on me as I tried to understand their lives. They understood that things changed so quickly in West Africa that an emergency could descend upon them and they would be forced to use whatever assets were available even if it was money intended to save their little daughter. I looked at the mother as she cupped my hand. She was comforting me in silence while I tried to digest what was and what was to be. I suspect she had been through it many times before, which made it no easier.

Knowing all of this makes little difference to how I feel. The reality is that I am powerless and a bit afraid. Afraid of a responsibility that I cannot take on and the realization that she is a picture in my head that will never leave me.

The little girl laughs as her mother holds my hand. She grabs my pants leg and tugs on it trying to get my attention. I look down and she points her finger up at me and laughs like little children do.

FIRST TRIP TO MECCA?

Journal entry
29 August 1988
Nouakchott, Mauritania

The plane is descending into the western section of the Sahara desert. At least that is what I have surmised from my map. Soon we will be landing in Nouakchott, the capital of Mauritania. The captain makes clear that we will not be allowed to disembark. We will be taking on some cargo, additional passengers and then taking off quickly. Too bad. I would have liked to wander some of Nouakchott's back streets. The plane's doors open and the hot desert air rushes in and makes the plane very dry. The bright light pours in as tall-silhouetted figures in long gown like clothing enter the cabin. They are all black men dressed in white linen. They quietly find their seats, one of them next to me. They all have small cups that they are spitting in. They are fasting. Is it Ramadan? I don't think so. Maybe they are making the Haj to Mecca. The plane takes off and after a short time the man next to me asks or I should say, attempts to ask the steward what direction is east. When told he and his fellow Muslims get up, face east, place a small cloth on the floor and begin to pray. It is quite a sight. As the flight continues, I try to make a connection with the man. He has a tall thin frame and long face with bright intelligent eyes. He speaks no English but tries to communicate as well. I think what I hear him speaking is Hasaniya Arabic but how would I know? To my shame I do not understand Arabic, any Arabic. Kris tells me that there are a number of languages in Mauritania like Wolof and Pular and something called Soninke all of which are of no help to me. The stewardess asks me what I would like for an early dinner. I say salmon and a glass of burgundy. The food comes and my fasting neighbor still spitting in his little cup looks at it somewhat longingly. I am embarrassed and try some French.

"*Jui suis désolé.*" I say.

"*Pas de problem.*" He answers. Finally, a connection. I eat some food turn back to him and ask,

"So, first trip to Mecca?"

Letter
Dr. David and Mrs. Betty Boyd, Edinburgh, Scotland
13 October 2006 Month of Ramadan
Tangier, Morocco

Some weeks ago I traveled from Paris to Normandy. I went to Colleville sur Mer and Omaha and Utah beaches. The wide beaches were nearly deserted when I walked their length. I tried to imagine how it was on that first day, as from the high hills munitions rained down on the first landing of men. Terrifying really.

Ten days before my trip to Normandy I had a chance meeting with an elderly man in Paris at Luxembourg Gardens. The event was the 150th anniversary of the Society of Bee Keepers. It was an interesting and charming presentation. As I neared the end of the exhibition, a small man introduced himself. His name is Yves. Yves explained that he was a beekeeper and a teacher of beekeeping to children. He had also built the wonderful models in the exhibition. Yves is a small man with a pleasant face and gentle spirit. It seems right that he is a beekeeper. After he and Kris and I had talked for a time, I thanked him and turned to leave. Yves then asked if I was an American. I said, "Yes." He told me that he had been a boy of seven in Normandy on D-Day. His eyes then filled with emotion, he grabbed my hand and said,

"I remember. I remember and it is I who thanks you." I was speechless, very moved and confess to some emotion as well. I just hugged Yves as he wiped his eyes. For a brief moment a man from the past came into my present and reminded me of another America now gone.

I thought of Yves as I walked the Normandy beaches and at Colleville sur Mer as I sat among the American dead. I heard someone say that the Bush administration and Congress had degraded all of the sacrifices of those buried here. I did not know if that was true. What I did know was true however, was that when the United States weakens the Geneva Conventions and agrees to a policy of institutional torture, my country then insults and betrays all of the sacrifices that were and are being made. I am profoundly ashamed.

Journal entry
12 December 2004
Dorset, England

After many false starts over a number of years, I am finally on my way
to Clouds Hill, T.E. Lawrence's cottage. The cabdriver knows where it is
and as we drive through the countryside he points to the road that leads
to Thomas Hardy's home. We turn another corner and the countryside
reveals itself with a quiet and subdued beauty. I can see that Kris is taken
with the land as well. The driver talks on as I look out the window
and imagine Lawrence riding his powerful Brough Superior motorcycle
fast down these narrow country roads. It must have been exhilarating.
I wondered, was he finally at peace on that last day in May, 1935 ? Was
he enjoying the ride back to the cottage from the post office? Did
he dream of deserts? Perhaps he was depressed as some of his letters
suggested or maybe he came to despise the hunger that made him desire
more and more pain.

"Here we are," says the driver waking me from my daydream.
The very kind Mr. Peter Preen, who takes care of the cottage, has been
kind enough to open it for Kris and me. As I walk around the house and
step toward the small front door, I see that over the doorway the lintel
is carved with Greek words. Their loose translation is "I don't care" or
"Why worry?" Mr. Preen first shows me the book room. It is a very
comfortable space with a fireplace with fenders designed by Lawrence,
bookshelves and a large bed covered in cowhide in front of a set of large
windows. I learn that after his death his library was sold off but when
he was here he had volumes of Greek and Latin and French. There were
inscribed copies by Churchill, E.M Forster, Siegfried Sassoon, Robert
Graves, Joseph Conrad, Thomas Hardy, George Bernard Shaw and H.G.
Wells, to name a few.

I went upstairs and it was there that I could sense Lawrence. The
music room was Spartan but very pleasant. There was a gramophone, a
fireplace, his writing desk and a comfortable leather sofa. There was a
painting by Gilbert Spencer that was supposed to be a view from 'the
crest' of Clouds Hill. In this room Lawrence would entertain friends like

Charlotte and George Bernard Shaw, Thomas Hardy and old military friends. He would listen to Mozart and Beethoven, Bach and Sir Edward Elgar. I could easily imagine him here with his friends listening to music or engaged in conversation. At the desk I tried to understand how it must have been trying to rewrite *Seven Pillars of Wisdom* after supposedly losing the first draft at a train station. As I moved around the room, I felt something else, too. I felt a profound sadness, a depression of sorts. Was it in this room that he carried out his elaborate charade? The man who came to beat him, did he beat Lawrence here? As I stood in the room, I so much wished that after those beatings Lawrence had found some measure of release or peace, but the strong feeling suggested otherwise. Perhaps the violation at Deraa was real and had awakened something in Lawrence that he found unacceptable yet compulsively yielded to again and again. None of this altered my respect and appreciation of a remarkable man. It only made him more real for me, a human being instead of a legend. As a boy Lawrence helped a solitary little boy dream of deserts and faraway places but as I grew older and read more I realized that he was much more than a facilitator of a little boy's dreams. He was a man of great substance, intellect, curiosity and inventiveness as the water system he developed at Clouds Hill demonstrates. Oh how we could use his intellect and experience now. What would he say of Iraq today? In August 1917 Lawrence wrote: "Do not try to do too much with your own hands. Better the Arabs do it tolerable than that you do it perfectly. It is their war, and you are to help them, not to win it for them. Actually, also, under the very odd conditions of Arabia, your practical work will not be as good as, perhaps, you think it is."

I wish we had Lawrence's experience and insight now, when we very much need it.

A PLACE THAT HAS WHORED ITSELF

Letter
Barbara Stone, Carmel, California
7 October 2006
Gibraltar

Dear Barbara,
Gibraltar is a place I hope never to see again. It is what I most despise, a place that has whored itself for 'tour bus' tourists. I returned to Algeciras and wandered the docks at night with men playing cards and women offering affection. Nice to be in a real place again.

A GATHERING STORM

Journal Entry
6 October 2004
Paris

There is no choice. I must do the laundry if I am ever going to be allowed anywhere where people gather again. I'm reading a book on Wilfred Thesiger's travels waiting for the washing machine to inform me that I may graduate to the dryer. A young woman in her thirties, I'd guess, is talking on her cell phone. After a short time the woman strikes up a conversation.

"*Bonjour,*" she says.

"*Bonjour.*"

"Are you Canadian?" she asks in perfect English.

"No. I'm American."

Her name is N and she is a graduate of the Sorbonne. In addition to French and English, she speaks Arabic, Portuguese and Spanish. She has lived in France most of her life but is from Algeria. She is bright and engaging and very interested in America. She tells me that France for all of its talk of humanity and equality is a racist nation. She says this with no anger at all, rather like a sociologist making a detached assessment after years of research. She tells me that even with all of her degrees (two in international finance) and multiple language skills that the only work that she has been able to find is that of a waitress. She said she has been to many interviews and all seems to go well until they see her full name and her dark complexion. From just a few minutes conversation I can see that in an interview she would be poised, professional and impressive.

"I hope that you don't mind me asking you a few personal questions. You see I am always trying to understand things and I always ask many questions, some people say too many. This is how I learn. Would you mind?"

Amazingly she anticipates my question.

"I am a Muslim woman," she says, "but I refuse to wear the veil. It is a symbol and a device to control women. All societies repress women."

"Some repress more than others do they not?" I ask.

"Of course. I would not wish to live anywhere that took my choice or freedoms away."

"Can you tell me something about the women who live in France or England who choose to cover in a free society?"

"This is what so many people do not understand in the West." She said. "What do you mean by freedom?"

"I suppose I mean choice. Are you not a "*femme liberé?*" I ask.

"No, I'm a human *liberé*. Look, it is far easier to comply than to be a revolutionary. Many of these women in France and England or the United States may live in a free country but they still have family, boyfriends and friends to contend with. If these people are always putting pressure on them, they just want everyone to keep quiet and leave them alone and the way they get them to leave them alone is to put the veil on."

"So it is not the woman's choice."

"No, many times it is not the woman's choice."

"That seems unjust to me."

"Anytime anyone's freedom is taken away it is unjust."

As the conversation continued, she talked about her love of jazz and dance and other art forms. She talked of her dreams and of her realities and I thought, a number of times, what a remarkable young woman. Our time together reminded me that in many parts of the world, covered and hidden, young women like N dream of lives with possibilities and the freedom to choose. I could not help but wonder if behind the millions of covered faces a gathering storm is approaching.

THE BEST BAD TEA IN THE WORLD

Journal Entry
13 August 1988
Manjama, West Africa

It is early and already humid when I set out for Manjama. It is the rainy season here with occasional gray skies and, well, rain. The walk to Manjama is about three miles along the main road, which is greatly eroded, and misery when it rains. You can walk for days here and never see a vehicle, only people with bundles on their heads walking long distances from one village to another. Many people walk the road barefooted and I am constantly amazed at their stamina and strength. Here I am with walking boots and a rucksack and I have a hard time keeping up with the older women. The small children walking the road as well seem to possess a strength that I have come to admire and envy. For people in the world who think that Africans do not work hard, they should come here to this place and work under the conditions of these people. Most westerners would not last long here. And yet with all of this difficulty, I am most amazed at their humor and 'get on with it' character and their stoicism. I respect them a great deal.

After nearly two miles I have become very thirsty. Silly me, I thought I could make Manjama in quick order and did not bring filtered water. I did bring my compass, however, so I will be able to calculate where it is I fall from dehydration. What a stupid arrogance on my part.

I have passed many people on the road today and we have exchanged the same Kono greeting over and over again until it is finally automatic like an often repeated chant,

"*En che na.*" (roughly translated, Good morning)

"*I kende chia?*" (How did you sleep)

"*Kase Yata ma.*" (answer, There is no blame on God)

Finally, I top a small hill and see Manjama. The walk feels as if it has taken forever and I am very thirsty. I arrive at my destination, which is the clinic in this small village. The clinic is just a cinderblock box with a part of the floor being concrete and the other dirt. The person who is in charge here is a giant of a woman in both character and size and she is a friend. Her name is Agnes Sebba. Kris is already there when she and Agnes hurry me into a room where a woman is moaning and then screaming. She is having great difficulty giving birth to her baby. Agnes shoves a big piece of cardboard in my hand and tells me to start fanning the screaming woman. The heat is oppressive and there are smells of blood, urine and chickens, yes, chickens are running around the dark room. They trot between my legs then scurry, as the woman's screams get louder. I keep fanning her and at one point think I am going to pass out, but then I get my footing back and concentrate on keeping the woman cool. I hear Agnes talking to Kris as they both try to keep the woman comfortable. Agnes and Kris are discussing something about a clitoridectomy and how it has contributed to this woman's present difficulties. Finally, after hours, the woman's screams stop and a healthy baby boy's cries take their place. We all are feeling exhausted and pretty self-satisfied as Agnes takes the baby and weighs him on her old hanging scale. I walk out of the clinic for some air. I am soaked with sweat, oddly not thirsty and a bit giddy. After all, I have helped bring a new life into the world and I wish him a good one filled with promise. I must say at that moment I was quite pleased with myself.

Outside of the clinic there was a line of women waiting to be seen. One woman was very agitated and the other women were trying to comfort her. Through her tears and shaking I could make out that she was saying that it was impossible for her to decide which child she would slowly starve so that her others might survive. Her sobbing was heartbreaking and I felt helpless and wished I could pick up that big piece of cardboard and fan away her misery and horrible choices. Just as I was getting paralyzed by the moment and lost in its inevitable tragedy, Agnes came out with a cup of tea. Agnes' tea was always the best bad tea in the world with its stale powdered milk and old sugar. I had always loved her tea because it always symbolized a kind of civilized pause after a long journey, but today the tea tasted bitter and I realized that no amount of sugar could remove the taste from my mouth.

WHERE ARE THE TAPAS?

Journal entry
15 October 2006
Madrid

Everywhere I go there are signs for tapas but nowhere have I found any that I consider wonderful or even good. I am in a sour mood. I begin to grumble that every place is becoming homogenized with mediocrity. Kris has heard it all before and gives me her stern sideways glance. She says we should try the Plaza Mayor and I grumble again about tourist traps and damn tourists and much to my discredit behave like one of those dreadful boorish tourists. Once again Kris' look silences me with a bit of shame and I decide, wisely, that I should just let her lead.

"This looks cheery," Kris says as she peeks through the door.

Like Dr. Jekyll, unable to contain his Mr. Hyde, Bad Michael reappears yet again and says:

"Cheery is not good. Cheery is for tourists who want to be entertained and have no knowledge of food nor care to know and the proprietors know that the tourists don't know squat about food so he sells them lousy food at grand prices and the tourists have their pictures taken with the proprietor and go back home and tell everyone what a mmmarvelous time they had and show everyone the pictures no one wants to see. It's about respect."

"Well we're having a bad day, aren't we?" Kris says calmly.

"I'm going in. You do what you like."

Grumbling, I follow. I hear Spanish being spoken, sometimes a good sign unless it's a lousy cook who speaks good Spanish. There are bulls' heads hanging on the walls whose eyes follow you like the Mona Lisa. There are hams hanging everywhere and there is beer, really good fresh beer and the tapas look wonderful. We start with the garlic shrimp. Fantastic. My mood slightly brightens. Then the Bravada potatoes with aioli. Wonderful. I'm actually smiling now. I walk across the room to look at the meatballs as the mounted bulls' eyes follow me. Their expression is disconcerting but not enough to not have me try them. Again delicious. This joint is the real thing and my personality is transformed much to the delight of Kris.

We have a conversation with an American who has lived in Madrid for twenty years. As he offers tapas suggestions, which are spot on, it becomes clear he has been some kind of special soldier. I have met these types before. His knowledge of history and current unfolding events and weaponry suggest military intelligence or something darker. After a few more beers I say,

"So you are one of those." "Yep," he says without saying anything specific. "I'm one of those or I should say I was one of those." He directs us to more shrimp and I direct him to more beer.

I turn to Kris, "Great place." She smiles and kisses my cheek.

DEPORTATION

Journal entry
10 July 2004
Genova, Italy

I suspect if there are more difficulties or perceived difficulties with Muslims in Europe regarding crime or immigration or just plain prejudice that in the not too distant future some country or countries will begin to discuss deportation of individuals. People have told me that that is crazy but I think it will happen within five years if immigrants and state do not cool down and try to accommodate each other. If deportations do take place, it will be by a country with experience in large deportations. In the recent past I think, lets say WWII. It will not be Germany or France, at least not in the beginning. Yes, I really do think it can happen.

Note: It is December 2006 and I read that the Netherlands is considering and may have already deported people. Even though there is great protest within and outside of the government, the government has said it will continue its policies. In 1939 the Dutch government set up a camp in order to assemble Jews who had entered the Netherlands illegally. Most of these individuals were deported to German concentration camps.

POLITE BUT NOT IMPRESSED WITH AMERICANS

Journal entry
1 October 2005
Istanbul

Took the little tram (the mouse) through the tunnel to Beyoglu and walked along the wonderful Istiklal Caddesi. Had tea at Makris coffee house which is pretty much unchanged since its opening in 1927 and then found a wonderful bookstore, Robinson Crusoe.

A very nice young woman named Nefin helped me find a biography on Ataturk. After much discussion with a co-worker, they agreed the best was by Lord Kinross. The young man asked if I could wait for fifteen minutes while he ran to the warehouse to get it. I thanked him and said I could return tomorrow.

"No trouble at all," he said in Turkish as Nefin translated.

While I waited Nefin and I struck up a conversation. Her English was perfect and she said that she had spent two months in the United States, Illinois. She was staying with her sister who was working toward her Ph.D. in engineering. She was very polite and shy and only after I had asked her twice to be candid about her impressions did she finally speak. She said that she was very surprised at the low quality of education people her age seemed to have. She said that they always seemed interested in sneakers and designer clothes or a television program. She was very surprised by this. She said that she did not find the Americans she met to be very intelligent or well-educated. She apologized for what she said and I told her not to be and that I very much appreciated her comments.

KRIS AND THE AMBASSADOR

Journal entry
March 1993
Freetown, Sierra Leone

Kris and I have been unable to get up-country to Kainkordu. People are saying that there are many bodies lying in the road. Kris is very upset that she cannot get more information and is determined to get up there. I have expressed my disagreement until we can get better information. It seems that the people are caught between two negative elements. If government troops show up, they say join us or we will kill you and your family, and when the rebels show up it's the same, join us or die or be maimed or raped. Trying to discern what is true. No word about Sahr. He is big, strong and smart and would have been a target of both groups. I hope the hell he is OK. I feel so goddamn helpless and pissed off but must control the emotions. What we do know is that we see truckloads of furniture and personal belongings coming from up country. They are government soldiers in and on the trucks. The sons of bitches are looting. Have they murdered people, the people we know?

We are invited to the ambassador's home for dinner. The Ambassador, Laura Lee Peters, is a tough looking woman who supposedly was an embassy officer at the American embassy in Saigon when it fell. Kris knows Kiki Munshie, the Ambassador's assistant. I think Kiki set this up. There are also some African intellectuals and a poet who have also been invited. At one point the Ambassador starts asking Kris what is going on up-country. Kris is taken aback.

"Don't you know?" she asks. Kris then says, "I'm not even supposed to be talking to you but I want the killing to stop."

Kris then asks the ambassador to help her get a vehicle so she could travel to Kainkordu or one of the refugee camps. She suggests to the Ambassador that they could go together. Kris is determined and I admire her courage and know if she goes, I go. The Ambassador does not say much after that.

A SAD ANNIVERSARY

Journal entry
11 September 2006
New York City

The city is quite subdued today on this sad anniversary. There's not much noise, an odd calm really. There are a number of events of remembrance concerning that other September 11th and Bush is here as well. I was here a few days after the attack and the city has recovered as far as stores and, well just pressing on and getting on with life. But something has profoundly changed and lingers. It is as if the soul of this place has been damaged; no, that's not it. It is perhaps the security that once was taken for granted is no longer or it is the pictures of that day that people can never get out of their minds.

I just can't get to the heart of it, however, what I can see with utter clarity is the courage of New Yorkers and it is something to behold. There are also remnants of the softness that I witnessed after the attacks. I don't know if New Yorkers see it, but it is there in the daily actions of the people, from the cabbie who talked to me, to the people at the University Club and the man at the British Airways counter who went way out of his way to help. There was the young white man I saw helping an older black woman who had dropped her bag of groceries. There are a thousand kindnesses that I see everyday. New Yorkers don't make a big deal about this. In fact, they may even sneer a bit, if it's mentioned.

When I get very discouraged about my country and can no longer find it anywhere, I go to New York and New York reminds me of what we could be.

MICHAEL AND HELEN PALIN

Journal entry
13 November 2006
Paris

Talked with Michael Palin yesterday and he is as busy as ever and in good spirits. I think being a granddad very much agrees with him and Helen. They seem endlessly charmed by little Archie.

He is very kind about my letters and expresses, a number of times, how much he loves receiving them and that I must continue my reports. Michael says I travel the way he wishes he could with no television crews or speeding agendas and I tell him that I would not mind changing places for a time and having the BBC fund my travels as long as I did not have to do anything for them. He seemed to think that was doubtful. I told him that Kris and I would be in London for Christmas and he immediately asked where we were staying. I said the Royal Overseas League. We often stay with Michael and Helen in their wonderful home, but Kris and I would never suggest staying with them during the busy family-filled holidays. Michael says we must get together but gently complains that we never have enough time. I agree but the time we do have together is usually wonderful with the trading of travel stories and, of course, the eating of good food (Helen's wonderful chicken dish that I dream of and can never get quite right myself); the drinking of fine wine and scotch and some laughs. Michael has always been a charmer for me not because of his celebrity, but because of his and Helen's utter down to earthiness (is that a word?) and their decent uncomplicated humanity. They live in the same home where they raised their children and they have known their neighbors for years. There is a steadiness and a grounded quality in them that I must confess I very much admire and envy. I wish they were my neighbors because they are good and interesting folks, of course, but also because they like and have cats and when I travel, I know Helen would check up on Ms. Thelma because Helen is a bright and charming lady who is a soft touch. The only problem with this scenario, of course, is the fact that after my cat had been cared for by the likes of Helen, it would no longer appreciate my homecomings. They are lovely people.

DANCING WITH DEATH AND MR. ROVE

Journal entry
31 March 2007
San Francisco, California

While watching the news over the last few days, I have seen repeated clips of the White House Correspondents Dinner. There is the President telling jokes about subpoenas while the Speaker of the House laughs. I cannot tell if she is really laughing or being nervously polite. Then there is a clip of the President's main adviser and strategist, Karl Rove, being asked what he likes to do in his spare time. He answers that he likes to tear the heads off of small animals. I guess that is humor in the Bush White House. Then a hip-hop song begins to play and Rove starts to dance. The mc yells, "What's your name?" and Rove answers something like "Master Rove." All the while he is dancing and singing, a well-known television journalist is dancing behind him laughing and having a grand old time. Other people in the audience, including a number of prominent news people, are laughing and moving to the music as well. I cannot forget that while this bizarre party is going on Americans and others are dying in Iraq and Afghanistan and it all feels so unseemly, so profoundly immoral (a word I rarely use) and insensitive.

As I watched this display, I wondered if any of the parents who had lost children in the war were also watching and if so what they thought. For even a moment did it cross their minds that their sons, daughters, fathers and mothers might have, just might have, died for nothing? I hope not. I also wondered if when men were landing, killing and dying on Normandy, was Ike dancing the Tango somewhere safe and drinking with a bunch of scoundrels who in one way or another profited from the war. Watching the so-called journalists and power people drink, eat and dance, I realized that we are not in this together. I could not help but think of the estimates that have come out of Johns Hopkins University and the Lancet, which, estimates that nearly 600,000 Iraqi civilians have been killed. People, of course, dispute those numbers and I understand. If I were responsible for that much death, I would also not want it to be true. I thought about an Iraqi mother who had lost her son and what she would be thinking as the president joked and Rove danced and the journalists laughed. Maybe she would hate us, maybe forever. The grotesque dancing continued as I recalled the pictures of the murdered Americans in Somalia and Iraq who had had their bodies mutilated and dragged through the streets as crowds cheered and yes, danced. Rove kept moving on the screen and try as I might I could not see a difference between either savages.

GALLIPOLI

Journal entry
24 September 2005
Gallipoli

I drove from Istanbul this morning to the tip of Gallipoli peninsula – many lives lost here in WWI. Proceeded to the Royal Navy Battleship memorial. It is a remarkable memorial. Thousands died here and nearly 20,504 soldiers and sailors died at Gallipoli and the Dardanelles between 1914-1916 that have no known graves.

Journal entry
7 July 2005
Carmel, California

I was awakened at 5:30 a.m. Ralph was calling from England. "Bombs have gone off in the center of London. Unclear as to how many injured or dead."

I called Michael P. then Denise, Sarmi and Cherry. All are well but there appear to be many injuries and deaths, reports say in the Underground and on one bus. Possible suicide bombers.

CHOICE, WHAT CHOICE?

Letter
Nick Barnett, Los Angeles
15 August 2004
Rapallo, Italy

Dear Nick,
Thank you for your very kind note and I miss you, too.

I very much appreciate that you feel that I should return because the country needs people like Kris and me at this difficult time. Sadly, I must disagree.

I think you know that the United States has not wanted people like me for a very long time. I know you keep holding up the Democratic Party as something that still offers a counter to Bush because you have faith. I do not. It seems to me that both parties are not interested in dissent and demand loyalty over conscience, which, you know I abhor. I find it counter-productive to 'goosestep' to anyone's march if that means I must forfeit an open and questioning mind. If you will recall it was 'liberals', in the previous election, who worked very hard at not allowing Nader to speak at the debates. It would appear that all sides have a bit of totalitarianism in them. You speak to me that compromise is not a bad thing and I agree but I believe that you and many Americans have confused betrayal with compromise. One of the reasons that the country finds itself in the position it's in is partly because of Mr. Clinton in the same way the left in France were responsible for Le Pen.

President Clinton could not get national health through but he could take one million poor children off assistance. He could not drop the embargo with Cuba but could pardon a millionaire criminal and promote, with great enthusiasm, a globalization that sent millions of jobs overseas and allowed corporations to run roughshod over governments. He could talk endlessly about economics but lost both houses and presided over an economy predicated on false numbers and stock market tricks and this in turn allowed the Ken Lays of the world to later destroy thousands of lives, and when there was much to be done, he acted recklessly and had his presidency neutralized by his enemies, so, I am curious as to what your definition of success is.

The great crime that Bush has committed has been to act overtly the way the country has been acting covertly, under a variety of administrations, for years, with all of its arrogance, criminality and brutality. He has shown the ugly face of America that has always been there and that others around the world have been subjected to but that we, the public, mostly rationalized and ignored. As long as we did not have to see its rawness, we could put it away and live with it. Bush, unknowingly, obliterated the myth and made us see our darker selves. One does not have to be a Ph.D. to understand this. Just go to Chile and ask men of a certain age to tell you what their lives were like prior and following America's intervention in their country or go to Greece and inquire about the colonels and the misery and death that followed. Go to Iran but don't mention that we wish to assist them in Democracy because they will then bring up the names Mosadeq and Kermit Roosevelt, the CIA and British Petroleum and you will have to explain why, when they had a beginning democracy, we took it away. We are still paying for that one as the recent September 11 report shows.

I have been asking questions around the world for a long time now and I have found that we have been laying the groundwork for the hate now directed our way for years. As you will recall, I talked about this in your living room over fifteen years ago, but Americans did not want to hear it. I remember you said something about me having too dark a picture of the United States and that other countries were just jealous of our success. And you are a very intelligent lifelong Democrat but where were the Democrats then? Where were they with Vietnam and Nicaragua and where are they now? As I recall, a majority of them voted for the Iraq war when they should have been asking difficult questions. And now there is a new political messiah (Kerry) about to be anointed by the Democrats. They forgive that he voted for the war and they hypocritically find ways around campaign finance reform so as to collect millions from some of the same corporations who pay off the Republicans *(la stessa minestra)*. The Democrats say there is a difference and they say 'trust me.' Do you really trust them, Nick?

Recently I read in the *Herald Tribune* that at the Democratic convention Gore scolded those who had supported Nader. How dare he behave as the "man who would be king," but this is the problem is it not? Parties and political people believe that the 'people' are there to serve and help them win. Winning is after all the American deity second only to money.

You struggle to convince me to believe in something and I do. I believe that people are basically kind and decent but as to my country I know that we have lost our way. I believe that we are at the end of empire now and surprisingly, I am sad about it. I thought we might have had more time, learning from history's past mistakes and abuses and evolving into something remarkable.

As all of the celebrities and political types gather in Boston and go to expensive parties and talk of defeating Bush and what positions would be given out for what political favors, my friend J sits in Iraq. He is a National Guardsman who is a graphic designer. A small life perhaps in the considerations of the big plans by the Republicans and Democrats but a life worthy of consideration nonetheless. I have heard none of them speak of such people or concerns. So much for a 'Tribune' of the people. It's all big picture and non-specifics. The politicians (Democrats and Republicans) sent a graphic designer from the Guard to Iraq where he sits in a trailer day after day and does not know when he can go home. In all of these Democratic and Republican festivities about high-minded plans and strategies to win, I suspect the fate of one young man far away does not carry much weight, but it does for me.

You tell me to believe, but I don't know what you want me to believe in. From your statements you seem to feel that winning in itself achieves something monumental, but unless the victory has substance, then we are merely talking football, and I have never really enjoyed the 'game'.

With respect and love my old friend,
Michael

NOT A REAL PLACE

Journal entry
March 2004
Carmel, California

We have a visitor from England staying with us. He wanders Carmel beach and says how much he likes the weather and the sea. He also seems to really be enjoying the cottage. At one point he says, "I would like to go to a bookstore."

"There is no bookstore in Carmel like the kind I suspect you're thinking of. We have a small religious, spiritual bookshop which, in most cases, would need to order books I think you would be interested in. The owners are very nice people but it is not a London bookshop."
He is shocked when I tell him that a larger independent bookstore is nearly forty minutes away by car. He looks at me and says, with no malice at all, "Oh I see. This is not a real place."

"No. It used to be something years ago but now it's just a third rate town in a first class setting. There are some very fine people here however, old timers who really care about the place.

As long as you stand on the beach and look west, you're ok. Only when you turn around do you catch an unpleasant odor. It's the smell of greed and indifference."

Journal entry
20 March 2003
Paris

I walked over to the rue de Rivoli toward the U.S. embassy. I was turned away by French police/military. I asked why I could not get access to my embassy. The officer looked embarrassed and asked,

" What is your business at the embassy?" As I held my passport up, I said, "You know that you have no right to ask me that?" He said,

"Yes, but I must ask."

He was very polite and seemed uncomfortable denying me access. Two young Americans approached us with their French friend. They were scared, especially the young girl. They said they had heard that we were on 'high alert'. I saw how frightened the young girl was and told her that all would be well and not to get too worked up. It was a serious time but they were probably safer in Paris than in New York. They should have a cup of tea somewhere and if there were any problems they should approach a police officer.

"Why won't they let us get to our embassy?" she cried.

Then, the French officer told us that they had orders from the embassy not to let anyone through not even Americans. The young couple became more frightened. Kris talked and calmed them down and then they left for a café with their friend as we had suggested.

I went around the other street and with bravado approached the biggest and toughest guard I could find. I held up my passport and old press credentials.

"I was told by the officer on the other side to see you so as to access my embassy."

"What is your business there?" he asked.

"My own business." I answered.

To Kris' and my shock we were let through with no one checking my large camera bag or her purse. As we walked down the narrow street, I could see people on the roofs and people standing in dark doorways with automatic weapons and covered faces. I made it to the large embassy doors. I was informed by one of the guards that the embassy was closed.

"What do you mean the embassy is closed?"

"It's closed," he said again.

"I would like to speak to a public information officer."

"We are trying to protect the embassy," he said sharply.

"From Americans?"

"From everybody," he said.

"There are some scared American kids at the end of the street who could use some assistance."

"They can access the embassy's web site."

"Then what?"

"Then they will know what to do." He said sharply.

"So I cannot see a public information officer or anyone?"

"That's right, nobody is here." (There was much activity going on behind him so obviously someone was there.)

" Let me see if I've got this straight. While we are bombing Iraq and American men and women are dying in battle, the U.S. Embassy in Paris is protecting itself from Americans. Is it not your job to provide assistance to Americans?"

"I don't have time for this."

"I know that you are very busy protecting the embassy but it appears quite cowardly being closed. Do you think the British embassy is open?"

"I don't know."

With that he pushes the big door closed and there, taped on the door front, was a small sheet of paper that said something like 'If you have any difficulties please access the embassy web site.'

I called later that day to find that the British embassy was open. I told the woman on the phone that the U.S. Embassy was closed and she said, "We are not responsible for what the U.S. embassy does or does not do." I said that I was concerned about the current situation and was it possible for me, seeing that the U.S. embassy was closed with no statement as to when it would reopen, if I could talk with a public information officer at the British embassy. She said, "We are very busy as you can imagine. If you do not mind a possibly long wait you are most welcome."

Journal entry
28 September 2001
New York City

Like millions of people around the world, the events of September 11, 2001, in New York City, Virginia, and Pennsylvania left me saddened, confused and numb. After seeing the pictures of the tragedies repeated on the television networks, I wondered if the country or I had changed in some way. On September 14, I set out across America to find out. I wanted to know if the country could be as reflective as it was reactive, or if we could discuss why this had happened, and whether or not our actions in other parts of the world had somehow contributed to this misery here at home. After twelve days on the road, I have more questions than answers and instead of seeking to find if the country had changed, I realized that the real question was whether we as a country have the ability to change and adapt.

As I traveled through nine states photographing and talking to people from various walks of life, I saw that the American flag had taken on many symbols. For some who felt helpless, the flag was a means of expressing support for the country. For others the flag was used to intimidate those who looked to be 'different', and for the intimidated, it was something to hide behind, as if to say, "I, too, am an American." Many stores used the flag as a backdrop display, reminding people that it is patriotic to spend. I wonder if we as a people are able to define ourselves as more than consumers or determine at our core what we stand for. As I drove through the west and Midwest, I listened to Christian radio (sometimes it was hard to get anything else) and the demagogues who sounded identical to the extremist Muslims we are now preparing to act against. In a small western town a woman wrote a letter to the local paper proudly agreeing with Jerry Falwell. Most disturbing was the blind and grotesque patriotism I witnessed outside of Chicago. It was the kind of patriotism that demands loyalty over conscience and always hastens a civil society's end. It is also true that there were many rational and decent voices as well like that of the World War II veteran who spoke to me at the Breakfast Nook in Rapid City, South Dakota.

"We can never kill innocent people or take away people's rights," he told me.

Though I have heard rational and decent voices and seen the heroism of ordinary people, I have come away from this trip unsettled. If we as a country and a people wish to honor the dead, then we must tell the truth, not only about the terrorists and terrorist acts but about ourselves.

A SEARCH FOR GOD? PERHAPS NOT

Letter
C.C., London
18 October 2004
Rapallo

Dear C,

I'm sorry that we did not get a chance to really talk. I suspect you have much to say about Bush, America and the upcoming presidential election. I would have liked to have heard your views.

I am just now settling down after reading the enclosed article ('*Cast Your Vote and Be Damned*', Maureen Dowd, *International Herald Tribune* Oct. 18, 2004). The commentary reminded me of our discussion concerning Mother Teresa a few years ago and I thought that you would find it of interest. I hope to hear your views before too long.

As you know, I am very uncomfortable when 'Morality' is raised because I have found that the people who talk about it the most are the least moral. It is used like a business card and is often a prelude to the most corrupt conduct. Take the current President of the United States. Always prepared to use the morality card to hide behind his actions which, I believe, to be callous disregard for human life and for science that might end suffering. This administration is comprised of opportunistic careerists who hide behind God and religion. It has always been so with the moralists.

Machiavelli wrote:

"We despise outward law, because our rulers are illegitimate, and their judges and officers wicked men, because the church and her representatives set us the worst example."

The inconsistencies presented in the article by the Catholic representatives seem self-serving and, perhaps, much worse.

As you know I am not a religious man nor have I ever known a religious organization or group to be on the level, or, for that matter, to be about God. Living in a Catholic country has been an eye opener for me. In the past I knew well the realities of the 'organization' but now it seems the 'church' is toying with my and other's futures and that is unacceptable. It would seem that the Catholic Church wishes to make it uncomfortable for the likes of me in my own country. Given the organization's history with children and the covering up of crimes, support of Hitler, Mussolini, and Franco, association with the mafia, plunder, murder (Roberto Calvi) and let us not forget torture, when knowledge did not coincide with church doctrine (Galileo, then, evolution now) as well as interference in the presidential election, it would seem that well meaning people who call themselves Catholic might reconsider their affiliation. It seems odd that supposed followers of Jesus' teachings would be part of an organization that, by its actions and history, seem antithetical to those teachings. I know that you would agree that there is a difference between searching for God and being a member of a club. People will have to choose between the two for it would seem that they are opposites in regard to morality. I suspect the majority will choose the organization. Tobias Jones writes in his fine book *The Dark Heart of Italy*:

"*Strangely, the immorality is also intimately related to the Catholic Church. There's a confessionalism in which it doesn't matter what you do, whether you're good or bad, as long as you remain 'in the ranks', as long as you profess your intention to get better. Italian Catholicism is all embracing (the origin of the word, Katholikos, implies exactly that): everyone is included, which means that everyone's forgiven, pardoned. There's nothing that a humble nod towards the purple cassocks or judicial 'togas' can't resolve. Politicians may be criminals, everyone may even acknowledge as much, but it doesn't matter: everything is whitewashed. History, personal or political, is quickly forgotten*".

I don't think that it is difficult to argue that the Catholic Organization is a criminal enterprise as are a number of other religious organizations like the Greek Orthodox church in which I was raised. The puzzle for me has always been how otherwise good people would associate with such an organization. If one calls him/herself a Catholic, it would seem, no matter how an individual nuances it, that they own all of the church's actions done in God's and their own name not just the parts they have edited for themselves. I suspect if one were a fascist but claimed that 'they' were a different, more just and kind fascist a fair question would be, why are you using the label at all then? Why is it necessary to be a fascist if your 'morality' is not in line with the doctrine you identify with yourself?"

Most people would not accept such empty rationalizations and would see them for what they are. In the case of Catholics I believe the same is true. The world is now inundated with extremists. There are the 'Evangelicals' and the 'Islamacists.' There are the Neo-cons (right wing authoritarians). The Palestinians and the Israelis. And there are the Catholics. In the enclosed article Bruce Bartlett, a former adviser to Ronald Reagan says of George W. Bush:

"He believes you have to kill them all. They can't be persuaded, that they're extremists, driven by a dark vision. He understands them because he's just like them."

Given the history of the church in backing some of the most reprehensible zealots of the 20th century, it's not so surprising that many Catholics support George W. Bush and his abhorrent policies. Maybe it is because they are just like him.

I wish that we were having tea now so I could listen and learn from your perspective for although I feel I have the 'gen' I continue to retain an open mind ready to be changed based upon, not emotion or 'faith' but the evidence.

Love to you and R,
Michael

UNCONSCIOUS

Journal entry
6 July 2005
Carmel Valley, California

I went to lunch gloriously alone looking forward to my book on Roosevelt and Churchill. Three people were seated one table away from me and they proceeded to go through all of the sounds that their cellular phones could make. They talked endlessly about what they had bought or their phones.

It is very difficult for me to live in this country. So petty. People are dying and killing in our name and we sacrifice nothing. It is increasingly hard to feel sympathy for Americans; they (we) seem so callous, unjust and indifferent. We are unconscious.

A FRENCH TWIST

Journal entry:
8 November 2006
Paris

My favorite beggar is where he always is, in front of Le Dome. We no longer exchange money but engage in conversation. He says,

"Bush, Bush". "Oui," I say.

I go to my favorite bar and Michelle greets me as always and makes me a Kir.

La Coupole has no dancing tonight so they don't seem to be directing the single women to the gigolos who are often waiting there to dance the women's loneliness away. There is a celebration of sorts going on. The Bush administration's absolute power is now over because of the election and my French friends think that the Democrats will deliver the United States to a new golden age; well, not really, they just want to celebrate and hope for the best. Though I don't believe in either party, I'm prepared to celebrate as well. I hold my tongue and don't remind my friends how many dead it has taken for the American people to come around, or how the US was betrayed by the supposed, 'Free Press'. There will be time enough for reality tomorrow.

The evening rolls out Kir after Kir. I head back to Le Dome to find my begging friend and give him a celebratory five Euros but he is nowhere to be found. I amble into my Chinese restaurant. The owner greets me with,

"Bush *est fini.*"

There seems to be a quiet optimism in a lot of places tonight. In the corner of the restaurant, an older woman with an even older woman smokes a cigarette in a long holder and the older woman rips off the filters of her Gitanes. Why doesn't she just get unfiltered ones? Don't they make them? My *poulet avec haricots noir avec riz blanc* is delicious. I savor it. The woman with the long cigarette holder hears me speak English to the owner. She turns, smiles, and says,

"*Bon soir.*"

Everyone seems in a good mood and miraculously no longer anti-American. I love it and get into the spirit of the evening. I move on to the Le Sélect and Pascal, though in great pain with a bad back and having already worked ten hours, grabs my hand enthusiastically.

"Election." He says smiling.

"*Pour moi aujourd'hui une grande celebration parce que Bush est fini.*"

Pascal's face relaxes and he pats my shoulder. I can't speak for anyone else but I think all the joy that I encountered tonight is a kind of silent hope or prayer that no more people will needlessly die. But die they will. The Democrats, whatever the hell that means, will have 90 to 120 days to undo nearly six years of profound damage and cynicism. My money is not on them and I do not forget nor forgive that they, too, share responsibility for much of the current misery.

I heard President Bush speak tonight and it was pathetic. At one point he said that the results of the elections surprised him. I suspect he was surprised because he never cared enough to pay attention in the first place. Maybe now, in the early morning hours, it's just the liquor writing this and just maybe that is when I, and everyone, are the most truthful. If that assumption is correct, then I wish Bush could be forced off the wagon and then maybe he'd see the world more realistically, take responsibility for his incompetent behavior and wipe that disrespectful smirk off of his face. Then he might consider going to every family who has suffered from this war on both sides and ask for their forgiveness. Only then will I believe in redemption.

WALL 25, LINE 91

Journal entry
November 1985
Washington, D.C.

In Washington, at the Vietnam Veteran's Memorial, I made my way to the books that contained all the names of the dead. As I turned the pages I remembered him as he was and hoped that his name would not be there, but there it was. Wayne Douglas Stigen, Chicago: W25, L91.

The Washington monument and the Capitol were directly in front of me as I walked along the narrow stone path next to the wall with its thousands of names. A man in his thirties I'd guessed stood in front of the wall staring, a small boy at his side. They held hands and after a moment the little boy looked up and asked, "Why do people go to war, Daddy?" The man just looked at the child and smiled sadly. I didn't cry when I heard of Wayne's death. I think I just got angry, then numb and finally silent. As I walked past the endless names searching for Wall 25, I was numb and silent again. At Wall 25 I began looking for Line 91. The black granite reflected my image and I clearly saw my face, then, there he was. I stared for a moment, not at his name but at my reflection. I had changed; my hair had some gray and the lines around my eyes showed some experience and wear. I reached out to touch his name and felt he was the same, still eighteen. Young people who die are frozen forever in time. Everything around the names would change in time. The people who would come year after year would see their reflections in the stone, their hair would thin and their bodies would age. They would change and finally disappear but all these names would remain as they were, forever.

I touched Wayne's name and began to cry. I cried for a long time and the granite reflected my sadness. I was finally able to say goodbye. I knew he would always be here.

ALAN AND KATI LEWIS

Journal entry
13 November 2005
Carmel, California

This is a bittersweet evening. After nearly thirty years Alan and Kati Lewis are closing the doors of their wonderful restaurant, *La Boheme*. My mother-in-law and father-in-law have been coming here for decades and nearly fifteen years ago they introduced me to the restaurant. Alan and Kati have always, like tonight, made people feel welcome and served food of the finest ingredients and really cared about their customers, especially locals. I have been lucky enough to eat at many places around the world and for me, without reservation, Alan and Kati Lewis are the finest restaurateurs I have ever known. Quality and style define Alan and Kati in the way that pretension and affectation do not. Kati is a tall and slender woman with classic features and Alan is a handsome and fit man who seems from another time when people were more gracious and patient. They are both people of quality and taste who have always worked their magic at educating a public on cuisine and dining without the public even knowing. They have done this by example year after year. It is no small feat to retain consistency and excellence in a restaurant day after day, year after year. I once joked with Kati that I was now going to *La Boheme* just to see if I could have a bad meal sometime. I never did.

Alan and Kati have worked very hard and I can't really remember them not being in the place. It is a serious loss to this town, not just *La Boheme* but Alan and Kati as well. Kati grew up here and is part of old Carmel before it embraced vulgarity and became an old whore willing to do anything for the tourist's dollars.

La Boheme is a metaphor for this town, maybe even a cautionary tale. While change is inevitable, wreckless change is a choice.

Kris' and my meal tonight was, as always, wonderful. The wine Kati chose, perfect. Alan and Kati move from table to table as if it is any other night talking with people, making sure all is well. Then dessert. Poached pears. My favorite. Crème brulee for Kris and their remarkable coffee. Alan pours us both a glass of sauterne and I drink deeply for the barbarians are just outside the city, some already here. They have no history and no taste or graciousness. They have no Alan and Kati Lewis to guide them, and now neither does Carmel. After everyone had left, I helped Alan put up old newspapers over the giant front window. Slowly, with each page the outside world disappeared and for a little while Kris and I, Alan and Kati had *La Boheme* and its wonderful memories all to ourselves.

TRUEFITT AND HILL

Journal entry
3 January 2007
London

After four months of hard travel, I am back in wonderful London. I rise early and am off to Truefitt and Hill for a haircut and shave. Being around for 200 years these folks know a few things about making a man feel renewed. Michael gives me an excellent haircut and head massage. Next, the young lady handles a straight razor better than I ever could and makes my face as smooth as a baby's rump. I love coming off hard journeys with few luxuries and then pampering one's self in a place that does.

Later I return to the club and after tea take a long hot bath in the tub that is so large it seems lake-like. I settle back in the hot water with scotch in hand.

Tonight, a light supper and a play. I love England.

Journal entry
August 2000
Craig, Montana

It has been a fine day of fishing on the Missouri river with Patrick Hemingway. We both caught some beautiful fish. The trout here give themselves reluctantly. Maybe that is why they are so appreciated when they finally take your fly. My face is red from the sun and I am tired in that very good way when you know you will sleep and dream deeply. Patrick and Carol's home on the Missouri is a delight with a large fireplace and screened in porch. The comfortable home is a reflection of Pat and Carol. There are many good books and some great videos like 'The Shooting Party' with James Mason. There are fly rods and reels, waders and nets in neat racks by the porch door that faces the river. I love this place. Carol has made a wonderful dinner of pan-fried lake trout that she and Pat had caught a few days before Kris and I arrived. Carol is a fine cook and the trout could not be better. I have another glass of wine and Patrick begins to reminisce about his years in Africa. It is fantastic to listen to him about his years on safari. He knew Bror Blixen, Isak Dinesen's first husband and the great white hunter Phillip Perceval who guided his father Ernest. Patrick's stories of those times and his stories of his father make for a remarkable evening.

"You know" he says, "my father provided me with a magical childhood."

I ask Patrick when he had decided to make a life in Africa? His bright eyes light up. He tells me that he wanted to make a life of his own on his own terms. His eyes light up again.

"When I first arrived in Africa, I was driving my car down a dusty road. I turned a corner and there, in the middle of the road, was a giant bull elephant. I got out of the car and just stared at him. He looked back at me unconcerned. I wanted to jump up and down I was so thrilled and happy. I knew I had found my place."

The evening went on with more wine and conversation but I could not get the story of the elephant out of my mind. I thought of young Patrick, starting out on a new life, overjoyed by the sight of an elephant in the road. He is an older man now but I have seen him with that same enthusiasm and joy hundreds of times when he catches a fish, or sights a bird or identifies a bug. When he talks about science or literature or mathematics. He is a man who inhabits his life. He is more often the student, always learning, but when imparting the knowledge that he loves, he is professorial in the best sense of the word. His wonder of the world is infectious.

I suspect that tonight, thanks to Patrick, I will dream of dusty African roads with elephants standing majestically before me. How grand indeed.

DOUGLAS HARDIN

Journal entry
22 October 2004
Rapallo, Italy

The phone rang very early this morning. It felt like a bad call and it was. Kris' father had died unexpectedly. Kris calmed her grief stricken mother and then hurriedly packed a bag. We rushed down to a frequented hotel and the wonderful staff helped us determine train and plane times. We just made the train to Milan. During the seemingly endless trip I watched Kris as she hid her grief for her father and the worry about her mother behind dark glasses. We sat silent and did not say what we both knew to be true, that our wonderful life in Italy was probably over as well. The train arrived and I got Kris in a cab that would take her to the airport for a connection to London and then on to San Francisco. I arranged for a car to meet her for she would be more than exhausted when she arrived, and then I called her mother to let her know that Kris was on her way. I felt very guilty that she had gone off alone but we had no one to care for Angus and Thelma. While trying to return to Rapallo, all of my efficiency and competence with Kris deserted me and after a few miles I realized I was on the wrong train. I finally discovered my mistake and after a short wait in a station whose name I can't even recall, caught the right train. Oddly, my compartment was nearly empty as I began to think about Douglas Hardin.

My father-in-law was a complicated man with a history of struggle and success. He was a decent and honorable man as well. We did not agree about much but I respected him and how he had conducted his life. In nearly eighteen years we had only one serious argument and that's not bad. Once he told me a great story about him as a caddy at the Wawona Lodge in Yosemite during the Depression. He would caddy the swells playing golf and then camp behind the lodge near a stream. He would fish and cook the fish over an open fire and then sleep under the stars tired and content. He told me that story a number of times and he always smiled like a young kid when he told it. He said he had been happy then and determined to work hard and make something of himself. He also once told me about his time in Hawaii at Pearl Harbor. He had been up in the hills working on some concrete fortifications when he saw planes flying by at almost the same altitude where he was standing. He told me how he could see the faces of the Japanese pilots and how everyone ran down to help the wounded and sometimes he came close to telling me how he had felt but then he would catch himself. I think the memories were so painful that what he had seen still made him ill. He had been a child of the depression and I suspect that is why he worked harder than anyone I have ever known in my life. Douglas Hardin had a work ethic that was astounding and startling and it continued throughout his life until today. After the war he came home, married and had two children, Douglas Jr. and Kris. He and his wife, Eleanor, worked and saved and worked and got together with friends in Fresno. After a number of jobs and owning a gas station, he went to work for the phone company. He was not home much in those early days because he was getting easements from landowners so the phone company could put up telephone poles. I thought of that as the train moved through the little Italian towns with wires overhead. Every time I saw Doug and Eleanor together they seemed very happy and content with their lives. They enjoyed the wonderful and simple pleasures of life. Friends, dinners, some parties and a nice drink at the end of the day.

I remember once sitting with Doug in front of a fire in the Carmel cottage that they had purchased for $19,000 decades ago. Doug was in his eighties then. I asked him when he looked at America today if he thought the sacrifices of his friends in WWII had been worth it. I had expected Doug to answer as the good conservative and America booster he had always been. To my shock and surprise, however, after he thought for a moment he looked at me and said no. I had always made the arrogant assumption that Doug was so focused on work that he did not reflect or notice the world around him. I was very wrong.

The train pulled into Rapallo and I walked the few blocks back to the apartment. Angus and Thelma were lying on the floor in the hallway. They both came up to me and stayed close. I suspect that the rush of us leaving with the bags had scared them. For the rest of the afternoon, I began to pack things away so that in a few days I could drive to Paris and then take a flight to San Francisco. The animals stayed by my side as I worked and for a moment I thought of returning to California and my heart sank for I had left my country with the intention of never returning, but now death, not desire was pulling me back. I suppose I was getting a bit depressed but then the picture of Doug camping next to a stream cooking some trout with his whole life in front of him made me tear up and smile. In that moment I could see the string that connected me to Kris and Kris to that place and that place to the stream. When I think of California, I will always think of young Douglas Hardin sleeping under the stars and dreaming of the life yet to come.

THELMA IN ITALY

Journal entry
21 September 2004
Rapallo, Italy

I never really appreciated cats until I lived with one and I was lucky to start out with a cat like Thelma. She is a perfect lady, though demanding. She is also a killer. Always has been. In Montana she kept our house free of mice. Then she moved up to rabbits and I even caught her once stalking a little deer that stayed under our garage eaves, now that's hubris. For over ten years we have been pals. We moved to Italy a few months ago and I do not think Thelma is pleased. Though we have a good size apartment with a giant outdoor terrace, it is rather sterile. There is no backyard for Thelma to explore and wander and as a result she has been showing her displeasure in a number of ways. So, against my better judgment, I have decided to take Thelma for a walk in the early morning. I have never walked a cat before. I use our Labrador Angus's leash, which is so heavy it kind of weighs her down. Well that won't work. Kris gives me some twine and with a smirk says,

"Good luck."

Thelma and I make our way to the end of the street and then across to the Parco Cassali. Thelma sees bushes and flowers and immediately tries to make a getaway toward them. She rolls around in the grass with abandon until she sees me smiling and enjoying her joy, which of course causes her to stop immediately. I take off her makeshift leash and sit on a bench. She sits in the grass for a moment and then comes over, jumps up and sits next to me. She's purring.

"Good day isn't it Thelma?" She keeps purring.

THE FAMILY BUSINESS

Journal entry
23 September 2006
Paris

A beggar on Blvd. Raspail is talking on a cellular phone. I wonder to whom he is talking and what they are discussing. Maybe he has a brother who is also a beggar (a family business perhaps). I imagine the conversation with his brother who works the Marais with a white cane and dark glasses.

"How is it tonight?"

"Not so good, only about forty euros. People do not concern themselves with the disabled like in the past."

"But you're not blind."

"Yes of course but the public does not know that. I tell you there is a cynicism and selfishness today among this new generation. It is very sad. How is it with you?"

"Not good. About twenty euros."

"That's not too bad considering you're just a beggar with a cup. I've told you about crutches or contortions on a dirty blanket or a dog but you never listen."

"At least I'm not like these new beggars who kneel in the middle of the street with a sign saying 'I'm Hungry' or 'Homeless Veteran Needs Work for Food' or the veiled women who just sit there and moan in the Metro. I still have some integrity, some self-respect. I've always been a purist, you know that. I don't beg for attention. I'm subtle."

"Yes, yes I know. We've gone over this a hundred times. The world is changing and we have to change, too. A little flash is not a bad thing and besides that kid in front of the theatre on Blvd. Montparnasse, I heard he made over 100 euros last night and all he does is kneel, motionless with a sign that says 'I'm Hungry.' Anyway I need to get off the phone. You know people don't like seeing beggars with technology or new shoes. What do you want to do later?"

"How about an aperitif at The Select and some dinner at Le Dome? Do you have a change of clothes?"

"Yes I have that new suit from the Bon Marché."

"Perfect. I'll see you at, say 10:00?"

"At 10:00 then."

THE ABBEY BOOKSHOP

Journal entry
December 2006
Paris

Today I spent a few hours at the glorious and wonderful chaos that is the Abbey Bookshop. I have met some of the most interesting people there including scoundrels and nutters, writers and would be writers, women and artists of all sorts. Confidence men and diplomats, you name it. The hub of this remarkable wheel is my friend Brian Spence who owns the shop. Brian is a handsome Canadian who looks like those old pictures of RAF pilots from WWII. Women gravitate to Brian and he, a romantic, usually succumbs to their charms. He is a generous man who loves books and ideas and always has time, and a bit of change for a down and outer or a hard luck story. The shop is small with stacks of books everywhere. It is what a bookstore should be. I suspect that a number of patrons have been lost; never to be seen again after an avalanche of books has crushed them. I do not remember a time when I have walked into the Abbey Bookshop when Brian did not push a glass of wine or coffee in my hand. He does that with so many people. He always seems to have some of the most attractive and youthful women of Paris working for him as well. This causes the bookshop to always be infused with a bit of sexual tension, which is anything but tawdry. It is exhilarating. Brian is a director in a fun-filled play that involves some very interesting characters. All of this should not give the impression of a lack of seriousness. When it comes to books, Brian is like a human encyclopedia. He has read much and when someone asks for a certain book, Brian can move through what seems to others as chaos and in short order retrieve the sought after book. Brian is a great hiker and reader of maps. He is a man of conscience and a guy with a soft heart for the underdog. Paris is a better place because of the Abbey Bookshop and Brian's presence. Long may their flag wave.

PINO AND BETTY GARGANO

Journal entry
August 2004
Rapallo, Italy

Pino and Betty Gargano have a remarkable provisions shop and Pino cooks as well. His minestrone soup makes me weep. Pino and Betty are outgoing and always greet me with "*Myco, buon giourno, Myco, bene?*" In their shop I have learned the differences among Parma hams. I have also learned a great deal about beans and the differences between fresh pasta and cold and hot processed pasta. Pino has so much energy and his laugh is infectious. He is from the south of Italy and in mannerisms 180 degrees different from the very stiff Ligurians. He and Betty make you feel welcome, so welcome I never want to leave.

"Try this," he says, "or this. Look at that cheese, taste it. It is from this part of Italy. Try this almond drink and this wine."

He says, "Come to dinner." and on and on.

Their wonderful daughter, Chiara, who was educated in England talks Italian to them and then talks the King's English to me. It's like a wonderful, grand Fellini film that is about food and life and family and friends. I am dizzy with laughter and stuffed from the food as customers shout their orders.

"Pino" I say, "I would like to buy some things."

"Yes, Yes," he says. "Now try this Cheese."

There is an explosion of life in Pino and Betty's shop. The olives are stacked high, there is olive oil everywhere and everything looks delicious. Pino and Betty have a way of reminding people how wonderful life is. In their company I don't have to be reminded at all.

HEY! WHERE YOU FROM?

Journal entry
November 2006
On Board the Train to Fez, Morocco

Young man comes into the compartment where Kris and I and an old Muslim gentleman are sitting. He looks at me for a while. I meet his eyes.

"Hey! Where you from?" he asks.

"I'm from Canada. Toronto."

"First time to Morocco?"

"Yes, first time."

"You like Morocco?"

"Yes. Very much."

"Do you want I help you in Fez. Show you the Medina and carpets."

"Thank you, no. Someone is meeting me who has lived there for a long time."

The young man's phone rings and he leaves the compartment. Less than five minutes later another young man enters the compartment.

"Hello," he says. "Where you from?"

"Canada," I say.

"Hey," the man says. "I'm from Canada too, Toronto. Where you from?"

"Vancouver." The young man's eyes widen "Vancouver?" he asks.

"Yes," I say. "Vancouver."

The young man's phone rings and he now leaves the compartment. After a few minutes another pair of young men come in. My eyes meet one of them.

"Hello," he says."

"Hello," I answer.

"First time to Morocco?"

"Yes, first time."

"You like?"

"Yes. I like Morocco and it's people very much."

"I have come back to Morocco to visit my family. I live in Vancouver. I am a hairdresser. I do not like men, though. Do you like men?"

"Do you mean gay men?"

"Yes, do you like men?"

"I have gay friends but as you can see I am married to a beautiful woman."

"Yes, of course. I am not gay but I work as a hairdresser in Vancouver. Where are you from?"

"Detroit," I say.

With that the men's mouths open just a bit. They then get up and leave. After they have left the compartment, the train is coming to a stop. The old Muslim gentleman gets up and stares back at me with a wry smile. I smile back.

"Fez?" He asks. I nod.

"*In shaa'Allah,*" (If God wills) he says.

NOT ANOTHER FISH
_____

Journal entry
7 August 2005
Craig, Montana

Patrick (Hemingway) and I walked out into the middle of the Missouri River. Amazingly there is no one. It has been a while since I fished these waters; it feels like home, like the first time. Pat moves further downstream and I'm alone. The water meanders around me. I look down and some vegetation passes slowly between my legs. It's quiet except for the occasional gulp of a trout or calling bird. I hear Pat in the distance and I see his arched rod. He lands a fine 18-inch Rainbow. Moments later I catch a spunky fellow of 13 inches. That will be it for the day. Not another fish. A good day.

WILL TAKE VERBAL ABUSE FOR SMALL CHANGE

Journal entry
21 March 2007
San Francisco

I'm walking down Market Street this morning and a homeless man is holding a sign that says 'Will take verbal abuse for small change'. I felt bad for the guy and thought, man, that's desperation. I want to acknowledge the guy and give him a few bucks.

"Good morning." The guy looks at me and says

"Can't you read the sign?"

"What?"

"The sign, man. Can't you read? It doesn't say anything about niceties does it?"

"Are you kidding?"

"Do I look like I'm joking?"

"This is strange, man. Here is a couple of bucks. Good luck and to hell with you."

"Thanks. Have a good day," he says with a smile as I walk away.

Journal entry
1989
Chicago, Illinois

I went back to the apartment after the kind people at the hospital said there probably would be no change until morning. I laid down hoping to get a few hours sleep when the phone rang jolting me up. The broken, gentle voice on the line said it would be best if I returned right away. I did not make it in time. My father died in that small intensive care room alone and I was/am sick about it. As Kris held my hand, I stared at my father and remembered everything he had ever sacrificed for me, and the years of pain he had endured as my mother lay dying. I remembered how he had worked so hard to help his little boy get through the death of his mother and I remembered his honor and laughter, his kindness and humanity. Most of all I remembered his unconditional love. Oh how I would miss that.

The tears began to come and nothing I could do would stop them. I smoothed back his grey hair and kissed his brow and remembered all that I was grateful for and so much of what I was grateful for was due to my father. After my mother's death he was determined that my world would get bigger not smaller. He introduced me to the Art Institute and Field Museum and Museum of Science and Industry.

"The world is remarkable," he would always say. "Look at how fantastic it all is."

My world has gotten smaller today and I cannot find the wonderful place that my father taught me to see. All I can see is my father dead today and all that I have lost. I know he would say, "Yes, yes Michael I love you, too, but go out and look. Look at how remarkable the world is."

ERICA

<hr>

Journal entry
9 November 2006
Paris

Today, at the Abbey Bookshop I run into Erica again. She is the Paris
bureau chief/critic of some art magazine here and we were introduced
some days ago. Impulsively she asks if I would like to attend two
photographic exhibitions with her now and impulsively I say yes. As we
walk through different parts of the city, it becomes very clear she knows
her way around Paris very well. This intriguing American woman gives a
first impression of a ditzy blond though she is neither blond nor ditzy.

We take the metro to Chatalet and there are some wonderful musicians
playing classical music. A man in a kind of black leather motorcycle
jacket is shouting at a woman in what sounds like Russian. The man is
holding her arms, she appears calm, he's crying. The cello and violin are
creating a bittersweet sound that is echoing through the tunnels. I stop
to drop a coin in the empty cello case and though the metro is packed
with people listening to the music or rushing about, I make out a quick,
darting figure approach Erica. He puts his hands on her shoulders and is
talking or crying. I struggle through the crowd trying to get to them. I
can't make out what is being said and while I see this as a threat, Erica is
smiling and calm. I get between them just as Erica says "*Da*" to the man
who then seems to relax. As I usher her away, she asks if I know what
was happening there. In a flip, snide and rather angry way, I tell her that
it was probably a hustle or a proposition or something like that. Erica,
who I now learn speaks Russian (not very ditzy huh?) explains that the
man was drunk and deeply moved by the music. He was trying to tell
someone how much the music had moved him and how happy it made
him but no one in the metro could understand him. She said that she
had not felt threatened and that the man was far away from home and
very much alone in Paris.

I was taken aback by Erica's kindness and humanity and the absence
of my own.

Erica is considerably younger than I, but today, she proved herself
to be the more wise. As we sat at a café talking, I could not shake the

knowledge that somehow in spite of all of my travels and learning that I had lost a bit of my humanity, or the ability to slow down and not assess too quickly or negatively. I could only hope that I had not lost it permanently.

MOROCCO, IF ONLY IN DREAMS

Journal entry
23 June 2007
Carmel, California

There is a bit of a respite now after Kris' brain surgery and radiation treatment. She has been very brave and funny and still tries to take care of everything, most of all me. I have been trying to take care of everything and her and now we are both exhausted. I have been sitting in Kris' garden and the warm sun has helped me drift off. As I do in dreams, I am traveling in strange foreign places and always with Kris.

I am far from Morocco today but it lingers. The Grand Socco and Fes' medina are clear in my memories, as are the faces of the people. In slow motion dreams I can see the folds of the women's long dresses moving in rhythm to their gait and I can smell the market's back streets where the camel butchers plied their trade. Sometimes, caught in the wind of wherever I am, I think I hear Arabic being whispered behind veiled faces and when the light of a place is soft, I remember the little girl with the gold earrings that caught and reflected slices of sunlight. It does not take much to transport me back to that place. I remember.

I may be walking down a London street and smell something familiar or hear a dog that is barking. What is odd about these memories is they are more complete and clear than I recall the reality being. The reality was that of looking at a society as though I was fully veiled myself seeing things partially with many shadows and barriers. In memories and dreams I am breaking through but in reality I never did. Often I would turn to Kris and ask what she thought. As an anthropologist she sees with a clarity I do not possess. Try as I did I never was more than a voyeur in Morocco. In some ways the people were not prepared and would not allow me to move beyond tourist or potential customer.

First and most importantly, my Arabic was nearly non-existent with the exception of my feeble attempts at *"In shaa'Allah"* and *"Ssalamu 'lekum"* or *"fin kein Ibit Ima."* But in spite of my lack of language, I soon realized that even with more language there was no guarantee that I would be able to penetrate any further. After my failures there I thought that I had left Morocco but Morocco followed me and now it beckons me back to explore other parts of the country and more of its back streets. I see Morocco as whispering veils and try, somehow, to make a connection, to understand.

IZ A MAFIA

Journal entry
18 August 2004
Santa Margherita

Giuseppe invited me to have a coffee with him at a café in Santa Margherita. It's a stunning day with shimmering sea and bright sun as I board the ferry in Rapallo. In very short order we dock and I head out. The warm air mingled with the gentle sea breeze is sensual. It is a perfect day.

Giuseppe is already at the café when I arrive.

"Myco, bon giourno. Bene?"

"I'm well Giuseppe and you?"

"I OK Myco, OK."

Giuseppe orders me a cappuccino and we begin our conversation with the weather, how the euro is doing, are there enough jobs in Italy and how well his children are doing. I am on my second coffee and he on his third when he asks,

"Myco. Why you have 45 million people in America with no health insurance? Is this true?"

"Giuseppe, I think the number is actually higher now but yes, it's true."

"Iz a something yes? You are richest country. How come this iz true? Iz a really something."

"It's very complicated, Giuseppe, and I'm not sure I understand it myself. Maybe as a country we just don't care."

"No Myco, iz a Mafia."

"No, Giuseppe. It may be many things but it's not the Mafia."

"I tell you Myco, iz a Mafia."

"Believe me, it's not the Mafia, really."

"Scusi Myco (Excuse me Michael). In your country you call them insurance companies."

"Giuseppe, I've never looked at it that way but yes, that sounds about right."

"You know," he goes on. "When you see a movie with Mafia, before they shoot man they say, nothing personal iz just business. Iz the same yes? When man dies in street in America with no money for doctor, insurance company say iz nothing personal, iz just business. That's a Mafia."

"Giuseppe, my dear friend you're right, that's a Mafia."

IF ONLY GEORGE CLOONEY COULD GO TO SUDAN

Journal entry
10 December 2006
Budapest, Hungary

I have been walking around Budapest today, mostly on the Pest side. My, oh my, bookstores everywhere wonderful bookstores and people here really read. There is a 99% literacy rate among people over the age of fifteen and they seem very bright indeed and very hungry, hungry to know and experience. I like them very much and I am struck at their sense of realism. The Hungarians are steeped in reality and possess a common sense that I must admit I find refreshing, especially after a recent conversation in Paris. Late this evening I recalled being in the Abbey Bookshop in Paris just a week before talking with a number of people about the genocide in Darfur. Many views and opinions were expressed that were grounded in history and hope. My view was that in the face of such mass murder, time was of the essence and that people must be made to stop even if that meant violent reprisals. The exchanges went back and forth and then an American woman of about thirty-five said that violence was never a way to deal with these matters.

"You need celebrities to help raise awareness," she said.

An Englishman who was present was dumbfounded.

"You know," he said. "This has been going on for a while now and much of the world has condemned what the government in Khartoum has been doing which is nothing less than genocide and the government has been unmoved. You're not suggesting that a celebrity could stop what the world cannot, are you?"

"You must try," she said. "Violence should never be used."

"Never?" I asked.

"No, never. What I would do is ask, lets say, George Clooney to go to Sudan. He might take other celebrities and get a lot of press and really get people involved."

"Get people involved how?" I asked.

"You know," she said, "to get people to love each other and stop killing each other. Maybe because of George Clooney, thousands of people would travel with him to really shake up the killers there."

"Do you think that in World War II if America had sent Clark Gable, Jimmy Stewart, Henry Fonda, Humphrey Bogart and Katherine Hepburn to stand in front of the gates of Auschwitz that the Third Reich would have repented and stopped their killing of Jews?" I asked.

"You never know," she said.

"Yes you do." I replied.

As I walked the streets of Budapest, I wondered what disease have some Americans caught that so blinds them to the realities of history and of the world. Maybe this is the way of all empires on the eve of their ends. Perhaps this is how they end, with rose-colored glasses that no longer register images of human misery. In spite of my disagreement with the young woman, I do wish it were so. I wish that George Clooney could go to Sudan and with his celebrity be able to remove in an instant all of the death and misery and fill all of men's hearts with peace and good will. Yes, I wish it were so.

Journal entry
22 August 1984
Crete

I woke early, put on my shorts and readied myself for a morning run. I have not always been fit but over the last year I have worked hard at running, have eaten well and exercised consistently without being a fanatic, I hope. As a result of the year's work, I am now lean, fit and very dark from the Mediterranean sun. I am still in my father's village and the surrounding dry hills seem to me peaceful and oddly familiar. Perhaps some cells deep inside of me transported there by my father cause this recollection that is not mine. I run through the town and some of the villagers stand in their doorways watching as I pass, then step outside to see me begin to climb the hill. A short way out there are smells melding together. There is the scent of lemons from the nearby trees, and goats. But there was another scent, well not a scent really, rather a sensation. It was a sensation of time past and present. As I ran on, I sensed a past. It was the ancient world but it was also now, right now. It was Plato and Thanatos, slavery and Democracy, lies, truth, life and death. I ran but continually felt that I was running in other's footsteps. Dust from the path rose around me, and I know I inhaled some of it. It was the dust of a thousand years of history. At one point I inhaled deep and in an instant felt that I was now of both worlds, indeed of all worlds past and present.

MYTH, DREAMS AND A NORWEGIAN GIRL

Journal entry
16 August 1984
Crete

It is late in the evening and I am aboard a ship heading for Crete. I am lying on deck and I can smell the Mediterranean. The sky is filled with billions of stars and I can hear the sea as the boat cuts a wake through the water. In Athens over the last few days I have purposely gotten lost in the backstreets wandering aimlessly taking in the sights, sounds and smells of the place. Yesterday I found myself hiking up the Acropolis and then standing at the Parthenon looking out over the city. My imagination could picture the senators debating or slaves attending to their master's wishes. Did they talk of the gods much? Sometimes I think that they had it easy being polytheists rather than monotheists. If one god were not particularly helpful to them, they could turn to another or still yet another. Was it a comfort to them or were they, too, filled with doubts? I wondered which was the myth. The United States where I come from or that place where I stood a day ago. They did dream well however, as their architecture demonstrates but they were, even with polytheism, possessed by their own brand of demons. Democracy and slavery, ideas and the fear of ideas as Socrates' death showed. They, like most human beings, were conflicted and kind, greedy and ethically scandalous and virtuous. They were everything and nothing and in the end unable to save and keep what they had built.

A young woman has put down her rucksack and proceeded to lie next to me on deck. Her long blond hair is tussled in the gentle sea breeze. She gathers it and ties it back in a ponytail. She tells me her name and says she is from Norway. For the rest of the voyage we lay close together, without a word, staring at the stars. Myth and dreams are hard to come by but are so enjoyable when they reveal themselves.

QUICK CHANGE

Journal entry
23 October 2006
Tangier, Morocco

The taxi driver has made his way through the city of 650,000 in short order, and dropped us at the fancy Tanger Ville train station. We are early and the station is nearly empty and quiet. The marble interior with its high ceiling is very grand and has a kind of mosque quality, which, the silence of the place reiterates. While we are settling into one of the chairs in the center of the great room, a man with taps on the heels of his shoes is walking across the stone floor and the sound of his metallic steps echoes off the walls. Like so much of Morocco I like this place but I really can't say why. Over the next hour the station begins to fill and all kinds of characters come and go. Outside a verbal fight has begun between a taxi driver and a policeman that seems to be about parking. They are just inches from each other's face as they yell and now others are gathering around them offering some views of their own. Making the scene even more entertaining is a man struggling through the arguing crowd balancing a giant stuffed panda bear in one hand while holding a little girl in the other. The policeman and the taxi driver are still yelling and now there are hand gestures as well, which may suggest a cultural escalation. My view of the outside goings on is momentarily blocked as a tall, slender silhouette walks in. The young woman with long black hair and Chanel sunglasses has a stride of assurance and style. She wears fashionable jeans, a cream colored blouse worn outside her pants with a black belt over the blouse that accentuates her figure. Over her shoulder is a tan leather bag and on her feet a pair of bright pink Converse high-tops. I watch her walk across the building and into the ladies room.

No yelling. I look outside and the policeman and the driver are now kissing each other on the cheeks in a most agreeable way. The other assembled people are smiling and begin kissing as well. All is settled and forgiven I suspect. Yelling, yes, hand gestures for sure, but apparently no fists thrown. How civilized.

As we wait my eyes wander around the station, which is now bustling with activity and I see a group of Muslim women sitting across from where we are. The women are in long dresses and their heads are covered, some with only scarves, but there are two women who are completely covered. It is an interesting picture. There are women dressed modernly as the young woman I had just seen and then there was the modestly conservative and then the strict with faces hidden. I thought how nice it was that all of these differences were melding together but was sure that in the end the young woman I had seen in jeans would become the norm. If given a choice, surely most women would move away from any kind of tradition or authoritarian dictate that would curtail their own choices. I looked again at the women across from me and began to look at their feet. How funny. One of the women wore a pair of Mephisto shoes. Why that seemed funny I don't know, it just did. Maybe it was how older traditions could accommodate some modern comforts. Another woman wore sandals and another a pair of black penny loafers. Finally, and to my surprise, on the feet of the woman who was dressed in light gray and completely covered was a pair of bright pink Converse high tops. Turning to Kris I say, "I have much to learn."

A SECOND LOOK

Journal entry
3 October 2003
Athens

I was last here with my father in 1984 and I remember being somewhat detached. I was younger then and filled with more of myself. My father is gone but I have returned with my wife, Kris, and from the first of my return I have felt my father's presence and have been remembering our time together. We hiked up to the Parthenon today and it seems very different from when I was last here. I suppose it is all of the work going on for the upcoming Olympics. Everywhere in Athens there seems to be construction and it appears to be way behind schedule. The little man asks me again for my ticket to pass and I hand him the oversized paper which he tears handing back a halved piece to me. I thank him in Greek. He looks up and his Greek sentences fly as I struggle to understand. He asks my name and I say Katakis and like so much of Greece he knows someone named Katakis from Crete. Am I from Crete he asks? No I say, I'm from America but my father was from Crete. He tells me that the people from Crete are strong and independent minded and that I should be proud and that I should never lose my language. I remember this as a boy in Chicago. The Greek community always wanted the language taught and used. My father had a different view.

"In America," he would say, "we learn to speak English." He always struggled with English but persisted and believed that English must be my primary language. My father was a very liberal man but once, when he came to California to visit me, he was incensed that voting ballots were in different languages. To be a citizen he believed it was essential to try and be a part of the society and a major part of that responsibility was speaking the language. As I said, he always had difficulty with English but he never stopped trying or learning. I thought of him as the ticket man went on about nationalism and language. If I chose to stay in Greece, I suspect that my father would say that I had a responsibility to speak the language. Kris and I wandered the Acropolis and Parthenon and I really saw it for the first time through her eyes. As an anthropologist she sees differently, more detail, more interesting questions than I myself would ask. She had me run my hands along the cuts of the overturned columns while a tour guide with a large pink parasol led a large group of Italians by. Kris told me that she was falling in love with Greece but could not yet put her finger on why. This evening we had dinner at a taverna at the base of the Acropolis. Above, the Parthenon was lit and the dark sky made for a wonderful backdrop. The streets are filled with people and it is 11:00 p.m. on a work night, no end in sight.

RAGE

Journal entry
9 October 2003
Crete

I was walking today near where my father was born. It is the small village that we had visited together in 1984 and for some reason today, I could not travel the last two or three hundred yards to the village itself. It is hard to visit ghosts, I suppose. Kris is gentle and encouraging but I could not or would not go further. I think I was set off earlier today when I saw a Greek Orthodox priest. In the background was the small white bleached church and then a black bearded figure walked past. The black shape was nearly illuminated by the harsh white background. The priest turned and gave me a stern look that I returned tenfold. I suspect he sensed my building rage for his pace quickened moving his well-fed frame down across an olive grove. His steps kicked up dust and the bottom of his black gown became increasingly freckled with particles of the dry Greek earth. For a moment I could feel hatred. As he disappeared, occasionally looking back to find my stare still fixed upon him, I was transported back to Chicago, back to the room where my mother lay dying. My mother was not a religious person to the extreme but I suspect like many people racked with fear and pain you reach out to many things hoping for relief and some peace rather than redemption. She had asked my father to call the local Greek Orthodox Church and ask the priest if he would come to see her. Perhaps it was last rites, I don't know. What I do remember is that when my father called, he was reminded by the voice on the end of the line that my mother had not tithed in a while and that she should first consider a contribution of some kind. My father was enraged and even I, as a little boy, remember feeling sick and angry and sensed that something quite inhumane had just occurred. I have carried that day with me since.

It was unfair of me to pull the priest I saw today into my past but he was and is a symbol of ignorance and self-interest of a kind I cannot tolerate. Ataturk had thrown religion out of the affairs of state in Turkey. He understood the fanatics and men of god. They were men; just men who had ambitions of their own which often concerned power rather than piousness. Greece has never brought their church to heel and they will continue to pay for that I suspect. Feeling as I do and with all that said, I felt badly about scaring the priest whom I did not know. I walked in his direction through the olive groves but could not find him to apologize for my rude staring. As Kris and I walked back, I realized that the bottom of my pants were freckled with particles of Greek dust. That was the only thing that the priest and I had in common.

STRANGER ON A SHIP

Journal entry
1 October 2003
On Board a Blue Star Ferry bound for Crete

In Piraeus we boarded this ship, which is part of the Blue Star Ferry line and have been impressed by its operation and our sleeping quarters. It is late afternoon as we get underway and Kris is wandering around the ship somewhere and I, well I'm sitting and writing near the bow. On the starboard side luscious clouds are illuminated as if from within and I am reminded of something I think Hemingway once said, something about dying young when you were most optimistic and when everything was in front of you and how it was better to go then when you were most happy rather than going on too long and being broken in the end. For a fleeting moment I understood but was pulled back by the beauty of the sea and how wonderful life is at this moment. It is getting oddly cool and the stranger near the bow has turned up his coat's collar. It is hard to determine his age. He is trim and has a thick head of gray hair and two weeks worth of beard. His features are chiseled, and he looks not Greek but rather from some Balkan country. He rolls and then lights a cigarette and as he takes a deep drag his face communicates a lot of living, hard living. It is a face I have seen before or maybe imagined, a bit like the world weary face that Bogart projected in *Casablanca* while sitting in Rick's, getting drunk after Ingrid Bergman and he had quarreled. The man, in front of me now, in dark worn trousers and an old navy coat, has that look and he reminds me of something else as well. How odd it is to be a traveler. The word always suggests a going to, but it really is a coming from as well. Where you have come from travels with you, all of the people and experiences, always. So it is today on this ship. The stranger reminds me of my father and of Crete years before.

In my father's village I met so many relatives but there was one, one that was like me. Uncle Michael spoke no English and I spoke nearly no Greek but we communicated in a number of ways. Early one morning a few days after my arrival, my uncle woke me and motioned me to follow. He was over eighty years of age then and still had a flat stomach, strong legs, a head of thick gray hair and a full mustache. I was in my thirties, trim and fit but not fit enough to keep up with uncle Michael who seemed to defy gravity as he ran over stones and up steep hills to where his goats were grazing. As he hopped ahead, he occasionally would look back and see me struggling to keep up. I once thought I had caught him turning back with a mischievous smile before, unbelievably, picking up the pace. He had deep green eyes and a kind of internal sadness that one sensed but could never really point to. We were much alike I thought then and I still do now. At the top of one of the steep hills he finally stopped and we sat on the edge of a stone looking out over a small valley. I could see the village below and the surrounding olive groves and lemon trees. It was like in a dream and I knew that my father must have come here often as a young man. Michael's goats kept coming up behind us trying to determine what we were doing. They nuzzled his back and tried to chew the small bag he had carried with him. In the bag he had some cheese and bread and a jar of lemon water. It was a grand morning and the simple meal tasted fresh and alive and real. We both sat there exchanging looks and then some laughs as one goat pushed me and then walked between us making a great deal of noise. It wanted attention and uncle Michael scratched the top of its head like you would a dog's and it settled down and soon joined the others. Michael was a gentle soul with bright eyes and a sparkling mind. I once thought I caught a glimpse of regret, not unlike my father's in his eyes, but whatever it was it passed before I could understand. I was well acquainted with secrets for there were so many and I realized that morning with my uncle that there were many places that I would never be able to enter and much I would never know. I had so loved the morning that without really thinking I reached into my pocket and took out my Swiss army knife and placed it in Michael's hand and held it there for some time. He opened the knife and slowly cut a piece of cheese, which he handed to me. For a moment he just looked out over the valley and then put his hand on his heart and then touched my chest. I didn't know him when we hiked up to this place but I did now. I think I even loved him.

The stranger rolled another cigarette and sat in a chair near me. He produced a bottle of something, looked over and made some gesture of hello and offered me a drink. I accepted and nodded a thank you. I could see clearly now the heavy lines on his face and his clear green eyes. Yes, his face was world-weary but the afternoon was beautiful and the drink in the bottle, while not lemon water, was delicious. I thought of Uncle Michael and I sitting together looking out over the valley as the stranger and I now sat watching the last of the sun moving toward its rest into the sea.

I'M WORKING

Journal entry
10 July 1988
Kainkordu, Sierra Leone

Throughout the week I have been walking all over the village looking and listening as life composes itself all around me. It is very, very interesting. I am trying to remain as unobtrusive as possible though it is hard to do so. While photographing I have, at times, heard some rustling and giggling from behind me. Turning quickly I have only managed to see the backsides of some local children as they scatter. Today I was having a very productive day when again I heard something behind me. I turned to see four little boys perfectly posed with makeshift weed circles being held up to their eyes. They were turning the circles as I turned my lens to focus and I realized they were imitating me. I quickly took their picture and they then made a sound of a click as well as if taking my picture. I held back my smile and joy and said, "Hey, boys, I'm working." Almost on cue they looked at each other and yelled back, "I'm working."

I broke into laughter as the little boys continued to look through their makeshift lenses. We spent the rest of the day walking around the village together with me letting them look through my cameras. A good day.

ADIEU TANGIER

Journal entry
20 October 2006
Tangier, Morocco

There are ghosts here like there are everywhere and the lingering presence of Bowles, Capote, Betty Hutton, the Beats and Burroughs has more to do with what I have read rather than a pitch by the city to promote those names for tourism. It is not like Hemingway's name in Paris which seems to appear everywhere to coax out the tourist's dollars or to elicit, in the tourist's mind, a golden time that has long since passed. No, Tangier is more subtle. Perhaps it has to be, for nearly none of the names connected with Tangier have the weight of a Hemingway, T.S. Eliot, Fitzgerald or Picasso and I like it that way. This city is what it is in spite of the writers, wonderful and dreadful, attractive and ugly, safe and dangerous. The city behaves as if it never needed the writers, and that would be correct. Burroughs and Bowles and the whole gang of intruders came to discover and take from the city. If it were not for what I had already read, I would have no sense of Hutton and her parties or Burroughs and his addiction. I would not feel Ginsberg's poetry or realize Bowles' élan.' I would just be left with the city and, for a time, the city would be enough, just like Paris.

I have heard it said that there was a time when anything went in Tangier. It is said in past tense, which has surprised me because as I have explored the darker sides of the city I realize anything still goes. I love Tangier, not like Paul Bowles perhaps, for it does not speak to my heart enough for me to stay, but rather I love Tangier like a traveler who has had a tryst with a remarkable woman and who admits, at the end of the affair, that the arrival and departure were equally satisfying. I love its dirty streets and mysterious alleys. One could be murdered easily here while the city and the people behind the closed shutters above me would hardly notice. That is why I like this city. For good or ill it is a real place that seems unreal given the homogenized world we live in.

Tangier is what it is, unashamedly so, but time and modernity are pushing at the city's doors. Young people are arguing about faith and business and America. They are like young people everywhere, hungry and restless. In that regard they are just like the intruders who came before when they, too, were young. From my short time here I can see that they are coming still. This time, however, they may succeed in stealing what is left of her.

IN SHAA ALLAH

Journal entry
12 October 2006
Fez, Morocco Month of Ramadan

Kris and I are sitting on a rooftop at night looking down on the ancient medina. The smell of burning charcoal wafts up and the sky shows some stars. After evening prayers and the end of the day's fast, people are out walking. Many places offer sweets and food of varying kinds. There is soup and bread, some meats and orange juice. People are talking and seem content with each other's company. Groups of women are walking together and a number of café-like shops have mostly men as customers. I turn to Kris and say there is something peaceful about this place.

"Maybe it's the absence of choices," she says. "There is calm in simplicity."

"Perhaps I would like to come again."

"I would, too," she says. "So, we will."

"*In shaa Allah,*" I answer.

CANDY AND CONVERSION

Journal entry
8 October 2005
Istanbul

Today I wandered Istanbul's large spice market. Most of it was indoors or I should say covered. What a place. Stalls everywhere with spices and candy and other items piled high. The colors of yellow, red and blue and sand even in the shadows seemed to explode. The people moving in and out of the stalls are amazing to watch as well. There was a woman fully covered in black that picked up some spices and brought it up to her veiled face to smell. One of her eyes caught my stare and she quickly put down the bright yellow powder but some of the powder remained on her veil and was oddly illuminated by its black background. It was strangely beautiful and made the stern clothing seem more feminine.

Hawkers tried to entice Kris and me to their stalls. We thanked them and strolled on. At one place a young man stepped out quickly and in perfect English said:

"Would you like to learn about Turkish Delight?"

The young man had such a nice presence and kindly manner that we agreed to step inside his stall and learn about that wonderful candy.

"You see," the young man said, "the Turkish Delight that all the other stalls hand out is made with sugar, regular white sugar. The finest Turkish Delight is made with honey. Here, first try this."

The man took us to the front of the stall where in a large bin there was the candy piled high.

"Try this," he said. "It is made with sugar. Now, remember the taste. Keep it in your memory."

Then he took us back inside and led us to the back of the small store. Out of a very different enclosed bin, he pulled out three pieces of candy as an old man drinking coffee and smoking at a small table watched.

"Now," he said, "try this."

I bit into the small piece and the flavor was warm and gentle and rich and luscious. It was nearly sensual and as the young man had said, very different. The pleasure on our faces made the dour old man smile and he shook his head up and down and repeated,

"Good? Yes? Good?"

I looked at Kris and could see she too was taken with the wonderful flavors.

"Thank you," I said to the young man who now told us his name was Ali.

"You are from the United States?"

"Yes. We live in Paris a great deal of the time but when in America we are in California."

"I have been to the United States, in Boston. I was in school for engineering but I could not afford to stay so I returned to Istanbul to help my uncle with his business here. May I get you and your wife a coffee?"

"Thank you, that would be very kind."

Ali brought us two small cups of rich Turkish coffee that was sweet almost to the point of undrinkability.

"Ali, are you trying to go back to America to finish your studies?"

"No. I will not return. At first I was very angry that I had to leave because of a lack of money. I was angry that America valued money so much and how it affected me. I was angry at a number of things."

"I'm very sorry that you had that kind of experience in America. It is true I'm afraid that America places too much emphasis on money sometimes."

"It is all right," he said. "I am no longer angry. I know that Allah had other plans for me. I had never been religious but then in America when things were not going well I met other Muslims who showed me some sites on the internet and I began to understand."

"Understand what?" Kris asked.

"I began to understand the one true path. You and your wife seem so kind and I am so sorry."

"What are you sorry about?"

"I'm sorry that you are both damned."

Kris and I were taken aback but not surprised by Ali's comment.

"Do you mean because we are not Muslims?"

"Yes, and it makes me sad because you are nice people."

"How do you know we are not Muslims?" I asked.

Now it was Ali who was taken aback and his face registered not relief but rather confusion.

"Are you Muslims?"

"No, Ali, we are not but for a moment you were not sure. All that you thought was that we were nice people. Is that not enough?"

"I wish it were for your sakes, but it is not. Here let me show you this website."

Ali showed us some extremist sites that wavered between conversion and penalties for a lack of conversion and the proper treatment of infidels.

"If I am an infidel in your eyes, can we still be friends?" I asked.

"I am still learning but I don't think so. How can we be friends and have such a gulf between us? How could I be happy knowing that a friend I love is damned?"

"What about women, Ali?" Kris asked, "Do you plan to marry?"

"Yes, I want to marry and have children. I will expect my wife to be fully covered to atone for my sins."

"Excuse me, Ali, but should you not accept responsibility and atone for your own sins?"

"No, you don't understand. Let me show you this website and you'll see how it should be."

As Kris and I watched this charming and intelligent young man move through the sites and go on and on about what Allah wanted and how it must be, I realized how the jackals of fundamentalism had preyed upon this person's disappointments and failures and convinced him that he was not responsible for any of that. It was Allah that had changed his path, which was now one of black and white. The jackals had removed all shades of gray and any doubt. As Ali went on and on, he seemed to get smaller and his voice more faint and I wondered which of us were truly damned.

NARROW ALLEYS, STARING EYES

Journal entry
14 October 2006
Fez, Morocco

I have really gotten turned around in the medina. I have stopped at a café of sorts to take a rest and coffee and collect my wits. For nearly two hours now I have been trying to extricate myself from the narrow alleys and staring eyes but continually seem to be pulled deeper into a complex maze. I usually love to get lost in new places, in fact I do it on purpose most times. I head off in a direction, turn, and then turn again, until my bearings are good and confused. Then, being lost I begin to talk with locals as best I can. Being lost is a good starting point for conversation because, although people may see you as a curiosity, they will not see you as a threat. But for now I am tired and my senses are overwhelmed. There are scents of cumin, curry and varied spices that I cannot identify as well as burning wood or charcoal. A worker at the tannery gave me some herbs to hold under my nose so as not to smell the brutal odor of the ancient workplace. Visually life is composing itself a thousand times a minute. There was the camel butcher making the camel head presentable and the sweets vendor who kept his eyes on me. My ears are tired as well from the endless sounds and whispers and

commerce. I am tired, too tired to engage in conversation. I finished my coffee and walked back to what at first seemed familiar. No, just another strange narrow alley with partially covered women. I walk past and can feel their eyes.

"*Salaam alekum*" I say as I pass. There is not so much a response as a murmur. Another alley and no, it does not look familiar. After forty-five minutes I stop for another coffee. There is a man with a small open market across from where I am sitting. Nuts and candies of all sorts are piled high in bins. Colors of red, brown, gold and green seem to explode in the diffuse light. I can see he is staring at me. I walk over.

"*Salaam Alekum.*"

"*Alekum Salaam,*" he answers.

"I'm sorry. Do you speak English?" I ask.

"Yes," he says with a smile. "I learned English in England. I went to school there."

"I'm sorry to be in your country and not speak Arabic. It is a very difficult language, especially for someone like me who is not very good with his own."

"You are Canadian?"

"No, I'm American."

"Oh I'm sorry. Yes, times are hard now. Please have some nuts." He then offered me some sweets. Thinking of Ramadan I said, "No, thank you."

"Please, you are my guest and you are not rude if you take a gift and eat it at Ramadan. We make allowances for non-believers," he said with a wry smile.

We talked politics, religion and philosophy. He is a wonderful man with a sparkling mind. As we talked I wondered if he were starved for conversation while surrounded by people who might not embrace his kind of open mindedness. When it was time to leave, I explained my difficulties in trying to find my way out previously.

"You are never lost in the medina," he said. "Look, let me show you."

Holding my hand he led me through an alley that seemed familiar and then one more. There was the arched entryway I had walked through hours before.

"Thank you," I said.

"I enjoyed our conversation very much. Please do return and

remember, you are never lost in the medina."

As I walked out into the crowded street, I discovered that I was no longer tired, just eager to explore.

RAMADAN

Journal entry
16 October 2006
Fez, Morocco

It is the month of Ramadan and this is mid-afternoon of the second day of my trying to fast. Yesterday I took no food or water until after evening prayers. The depriving of water was harder for me than no food and I grew quite light-headed. I am fasting to experience one of the Five Pillars of Islam and to try and understand what it feels like. However, I can only get so far for I cannot enter or accept the religious fervor and atonement that is the foundation of the fasting. Ramadan is the holy month of fasting. It takes place in the ninth month of the Muslim year (Lunar Calendar) and it commemorates the revelation of the Quran to Muhammad. During this holy month Muslims must fast and not take part in sexual activity during the day. After evening prayers the streets are alive with men smoking water pipes in café's and women walking the streets arm in arm in bright colored textiles. There was a good-natured commotion about the place. People usually broke the fast with a wonderful bean soup that I think was called Herra. There was bread and fruit, sweets and coffee; it was all wonderful and satisfying.

There is something about depriving one's self and then partaking in that which was deprived that makes it taste even better. This food tasted like ambrosia and I ate slowly tasting each bite carefully trying to identify the different flavors.

Sitting in a café alone, a number of men turned to see the stranger in their midst. One man nodded his head and had a coffee and sweet sent to my table. I nodded back and smiled. He simply grinned, lit up a cigarette and continued his conversation with the people at his table. I was well aware that there was not one single woman in the café nor for that matter one man, with the exception of myself, sitting alone. I tasted the sweet, which was, very much like Greek baklava, and the strong coffee that demanded a good deal of sugar. It all tasted so good in the exotic, smoke filled night air. For some reason I thought of my bucket baths when I had lived in West Africa. I had come to enjoy pouring river water over me every morning; in fact it was a real luxury there. As a result of those months of bucket baths, I remember returning to London and being amazed at how remarkable it felt to have a long hot bath with a scotch and the day's paper. It was as if I were having a hot bath for the first time. That is how it felt now, sitting in a café of believers taking a last bite of sweet and sip of coffee. It felt like eating for the first time.

FAREWELL SWEET SASHA

Letter
Patrick and Carol Hemingway, Bozeman, Montana
9 September 2006
Carmel, California

Dear Pat and Carol,
Kris and I were sad to hear of Sasha's passing. Memories flooded in and we both recalled her little wiggle when she came to you and how she would look in my eyes when I scratched her ears. She was a delight and, as you said, Pat, had wonderful manners. Kris and I laughed as we recalled how, when she was ready for bed, she let you know. Sasha always made me smile. She was a gentle soul who enjoyed her life with the people who cared for and loved her well.

As you know, Angus is getting quite old. This October he will turn ninety-one in dog years. He has lost some of his hearing but little of his desire. Even now he sits by the ocean and trails geese and duck and sniffs the air for scent.

There is a nip in the air here that suggests fall, which you know is my favorite season. In Montana it meant getting out the old hunting vest, shotgun and boots and readying everything for partridge hunting.

I went to the garage today and pulled out my old hunting gear and the vest that still had pheasant feathers in it and Angus sat close and then stuck his nose deep in the vest. His tail made a circular motion like a propeller and his muscles rippled under his sagging coat. For a moment he was young again and ready to go. He sat by my side leaning against my leg quivering.

There were many hours that Angus and I walked golden fields together. The weather would sometimes turn very cold and we would be in the middle of nowhere with maybe an hour's walk back to the truck. If I had let him, he would have gone on and on. Even now I know he would drive himself to the end. Noble friend.

When we finished on those autumn days, we were usually wet and cold and happy. Angus would collapse in the back of the truck and together we would travel through open country where the aspens, seemingly illuminated from within, showed off their fall color. Arriving home I would feed Angus, kick off my boots and settle in by the fire with a scotch. Soon Angus and I would drift off, I in the big armchair and he in front of the fire on top of my wet boots. I saw that look in his eye today. We were back in those Montana fields.

Since hearing of Sasha's passing, I must say I am glad she went the way she did, with a nice dinner, a nose full of autumn's smells and the anticipation of days afield. I wish that for Angus and for ourselves.
Love to you both,
Michael

A PERFECT DAY IN CHANTILLY

Journal entry
18 May 2008
Paris

I have just returned from an outing that can only be described as perfect. In fact, it was more than perfect and its memory, lingering deliciously, is still providing much pleasure.

Mary Fort started out as Kris' and my banker but became our friend. She and her husband, Gerard, have always been people that we have liked and trusted, and in the few times that we have been together, it has been a pleasure to be in their company. Mary is a beautiful Irish woman who, as a young lady, met the slightly older Gerard. Gerard, even as an older man today, is handsome, charming and very bright. It is easy to see how he swept Mary off her feet and after meeting her, you can also see why he would have wanted to.

It was arranged some weeks ago that Mary and Gerard would drive to Paris, pick us up and then take us to their home in Chantilly. A light rain was falling when they arrived and after exchanging hellos we began to travel out of the city.

It is very comfortable to be with Mary and Gerard, so, it came as no surprise that in a short time the conversation seemed to begin where we had left off a year before. We talked of French politics and of history, of food and wine and how we were feeling. We drove through pretty country stopping at the town of Senlis. During mass we went into the town's magnificent cathedral where people in the pews and around the outer walls were dressed as you would expect and some of the little children in their Sunday best tried to curb their restlessness without success. The light rain, a mist really, continued as we had coffee in a small café.

Arriving at Mary and Gerard's home, Kris and I were introduced to their daughters, Lauriane and Celia. I cannot explain what started to happen in this house. It was a feeling beyond comfortable, rather a feeling of satisfaction and contentment. The old paintings on the walls were done by some of Gerard's family and the photograph on a table showed a very young and handsome Gerard. The face was reminiscent of Marcello Mastroianni.

Gerard explained with great pride that this land had been his grandfather's and that he, himself, had done much of the work on the additions of the house. In fact, shortly before our visit, he had made a new outside deck in the front of the house. He talked with precision about his building the fireplace with some carved stones that had come from the time of the Crusades. At the same time I could hear Mary, Lauriane and Celia in the kitchen discussing the afternoon meal as Gerard went on to show me the one grapevine that his grandfather had planted. It all seemed so right. Every corner was who they were and where they had come from. It was a real home and I felt very much at home myself.

The tagine was served and Gerard opened a Chateau Gloria and other fine wines. The food was so good that Kris and I just exchanged looks with rolling eyes. The table conversation flew from racism to gay rights to the war to politics. It was amazing because Celia and Lauriane are very bright and passionate young people. They argued with their father and mother while both stayed calm but it was clear to Kris and me that Mary and Gerard were very proud of the children they had raised. These two young women were strong, independent and most importantly kind. Kris and I again smiled as Celia made points about a number of issues with which her father had some different views. Celia became more passionate and Gerard stayed calm. At one point, when the discussion got a bit heated, Celia turned to me and said, "You know my father is my best friend?" I had no doubt about that at all.

As the afternoon went on with wine, laughter and serious conversation, there were at least a dozen times when Kris and I exchanged grins. When we asked how often the family had dinner together with conversations like these, the two girls looked at us with perplexed expressions.

"Every night we have a meal together," answered Lauriane with Gerard, Mary and Celia agreeing.

"This is not so in the United States?" asked Gerard.

I watched as Gerard looked at me with a kind of sadness. I could feel that he felt badly for the people who did not have the life that he had with his family. Gerard is a decent and sensitive man who cares about the world because he knows well that his children will have to live in this world.

As Gerard poured a fine brandy after lunch, Kris and I sat next to each other on the sofa. The conversation wafted through the room as I held Kris' hand and looked over to see Mary and Celia, Lauriane and Gerard laughing. Kris squeezed my hand as she laughed at something being said, and in that moment I wanted time to stop and for Kris and me to be frozen in that time and in that place, forever. It was a perfect day.

Journal entry
29 September 2003
Sounio, Greece

Kris and I have hiked up to the ruins of the Temple of Poseidon and the sea opens up before us. The breathtaking vista makes clear why the temple was built here. If Poseidon, the god of the sea, had lived anywhere he would have lived here. It is magnificent and we are gloriously alone with these ruins created some 440 years before Christ. Kris is sitting on one of the massive overturned columns as she opens her rucksack and pulls out the small watercolor box I bought for her in Paris years before. She is turned sideways and with her large sunbonnet and skirt, in silhouette, she looks like a traveler from another century in one of those old books that you would find in London. From the day I met her, I thought her the most beautiful woman I had ever seen. As a young anthropologist she had just returned from living in West Africa for years. Brains and beauty I had thought at our first meeting when I could not find the words, any words. She was kind as I stumbled. She has always been kind. As I watched her painting, I could not help but think of all of the miles we have traveled together since that first meeting, thousands of miles. I have learned much from her for she is always engaged in the world wanting to understand that which she does not understand. She is my center, my friend and my True North always guiding and welcoming me home.

EPILOGUE

Deciding to remember, and what to remember, is how we decide who we are.
Robert Pinsky, America's three-time Poet Laureate

As a young boy I was infected with wanderlust. Is it any wonder really? As my mother lay dying in the next room, my father would occupy me with books and stories. There were *A Thousand and One Arabian Nights* and *Kim*, picture books with deserts and pyramids and my father's photographs of ancient Greek ruins and European cities at the turn of the century. There were stories of Ataturk and Greek mythology, of Lawrence of Arabia and maps, always maps. I also recall books with the words of people long gone describing a river discovered or a continent crossed. All of this fired my imagination. My father provided me with a magic carpet that took me far beyond the sadness that resided within the walls of our small Chicago apartment and in so doing there were many nights when I dreamed of deserts and of Lawrence or of India or Pakistan or Paris. In those dreams I hungered for the world. I wanted to know and see and experience. After hundreds of thousands of miles, I am still hungry.

Ernest Hemingway once said that every time he saw words it was as if he were seeing them for the first time. And, for me, every time I walk ancient streets or board a train or ship or plane the feeling, too, is like the first time.

Some time ago I left the United States never to return. It was death that first brought me back and then Kris' illness that had us stay. I returned to see the United States clearly, with no adornment nor fear and I quickly lost patience with the nationalistic pose that still contaminates not only the place, but also the psyche of the people. As I wandered the streets here, I began to recall some of my father's worries about the country he so loved.

"This is a great country," he once told me, "but they care too much for money here. I think someday money will be their final definition and purpose. You know, betrayal often comes from the inside and it is often for the oldest of reasons, greed. When it comes, the betrayal will be for nothing more than a handful of silver."

And so it has come to pass. With what I have seen here, I am reminded of what a Muslim woman once said to me, "One should never be a sheep in a land of hyenas." I had always hoped for more from my country.

Since returning, my saddest observation is that there is nothing America can teach me now. I am beyond its self-delusions and I can no longer be manipulated by its use of fear. To anyone who remains objective, it is clear that America has lost its way. Even now, as I write this, I recall watching the news a few moments ago. The President of the United States was joking and conducting the Marine band in a cowboy hat while the assembled media and celebrities cheered him on. I had hoped, after all that has happened, that the president and others would have changed, perhaps found their humanity and finally comprehended the unseemliness and criminality of their behavior as young Americans and others continued to die in Iraq and Afghanistan. As I have watched the decline of my country from here and abroad, I have been reminded, thanks to Sara Paretsky's *Writing In An Age of Silence,* of Richard II, Act II, Scene I:

> This land of such dear souls, this dear dear land,
> Dear for her reputation through the world,
> Is now leas'd out-I die pronouncing it-
> Like to a tenement or pelting farm.
> England, bound in with the triumphant sea,
> Whose rocky shore beats back the envious siege
> Of wat'ry Neptune, is now bound in with shame,
> With inky blots and rotten parchment bonds;
> That England, that was wont to conquer others,
> Hath made a shameful conquest of itself.

Our time is passing now and another empire is ascending. I hope that those who follow will study how we came to where we are today and have the desire and the will to find another way to treat the world and its own citizens. Perhaps then they will not squander their blessings nor find out too late that they, too, have sold their futures for a handful of silver.

3 June 2008
San Francisco,

ACKNOWLEDGMENTS

There are many people that I have encountered on my travels who have been kind, informative and, at times inspiring. While it is understood that real travel changes one's perceptions of self and the world, it is, for me, impossible to calculate or express how much these encounters have informed and altered the direction of my life. If I were to name all of those who deserve thanks, the pages of this book would be doubled. So, if anyone remembers me, but does not find his or her name here, please know that my appreciation is no less felt.

I want to thank Michael Palin for his introduction and his friendship. Our continuing discussions about the world have been going on for nearly ten years and they continue to be a pleasure. I want to express my appreciation to Mr. Peter Preen for opening up Lawrence's cottage (Clouds Hill) in Dorset for Kris and me and then taking us personally through every room sharing his extensive knowledge of the house and of Lawrence. Thanks to Mr. Collin Harris of the Bodleian Library, University of Oxford and to the dedicated people at The Royal Geographical Society, London. My sincere thanks to Ms. Carole Holden of the British Library and to Mr. John Morton at the Victoria and Albert Museum. To Dr. David Boyd of Edinburgh. To my Greek publisher, 'Kastaniotis Editions' who believed in Traveller early, in particular, Mr. Anteos Chrysostomides and Ms. Sophie Catris. Thanks to my Chinese translator Mr. Sean Lian and Yilin Press. To Tanya Johnson, a great editor and an even greater friend who made this book better.

Thank you to Patrick and Carol Hemingway for so many reasons and to Dennis High for believing early on.

To Ms. Barbara Stone who always has time for a cup of tea. Her stories of being a nurse with the Princess Mary's Royal Air Force Nursing Service in the Sudan, 1946-48 still excite my imagination. Thank you to Bilgi Kuflu in Ankara and to Nataly Adrian in Paris. To the dear 'Gang' in London who always provided shelter, sustenance and great conversation as well as much needed support when the skies darkened. They are, Michael and Sarmi Lawrence, Denise Prior, Julian Davis and Clare Gibson, Richard Fawkes and Cherry Cole. To Peggy Gotthold and Lawrence Van Velzer of Foolscap Press and to Rose Baring in London who believed and tried.

Many thanks to Mr. Nick Barnett for his years of friendship and support.

To Dr. Nancy Rubin for her humanity and kindness in caring for the person I most love in the world. I simply do not have the words. Also, many thanks to Dr. Susan Chang and Dr. Raymond Liu who keep watch over Kris and Dr. Patrick Feehan. My profound thanks to doctors David L. Smith, Peter Whybrow and Diane Strachowski who helped curb the 'Black Dog.'

To Gina and Nico Marrone and Pino and Betty Gargano in Rapallo for their hospitality and minestrone. My gratitude to DeWitt Sage who first saw the 'Black Dog' and warned me.

To my friend Sahr in Sierra Leone who watched out for me and to my dear friend Cary Porter. To Wendy Ellis Smith for her unending generosity and kindness during the dark time. To Dr. Peter English and to Marsha Shapiro who always finds the books I need. To Seán Hemingway of the Metropolitan Museum of Art for his encouragement and support. Thanks to Susan Moldow, Jeff Wilson and Lydia Zelaya at Scribner and Simon and Schuster for their incredible kindness. To Venka Ragina in Bulgaria. Merci to my French teacher in Paris, Monsieur Patrick Gremy and to Mr. Abdo Hage who assisted me with Arabic. To Ms. Jean Marie O'Brien, owner of the Old Monterey Book Company for *Crusader Castles*, merci.

To my dear late father George E. Katakis, a great traveler who, in spite of seeing many horrors in WWII, embraced the world.

Finally, to my 'True North' Kris L. Hardin. She is the finest of travelers and companions. To try and put into words what I have learned from her and what she means to me would again, double this book's pages. So, for now a heartfelt thank you and my love will have to suffice.